NEW DIRECTIONS FOR INSTITUTI...

Patrick T. Terenzini
The Pennsylvania State University
EDITOR-IN-CHIEF

Ellen Earle Chaffee
North Dakota University System
ASSOCIATE EDITOR

Developing Effective Policy Analysis in Higher Education

Judith I. Gill
Western Interstate Commission for Higher Education

Laura Saunders
Highline Community College

EDITORS

Number 76, Winter 1992

JOSSEY-BASS PUBLISHERS
San Francisco

DEVELOPING EFFECTIVE POLICY ANALYSIS IN HIGHER EDUCATION
Judith I. Gill, Laura Saunders (eds.)
New Directions for Institutional Research, no. 76
Volume XIV, Number 4
Patrick T. Terenzini, Editor-in-Chief
Ellen Earle Chaffee, Associate Editor

Microfilm copies of issues and articles are available in 16mm and 35mm, as well as microfiche in 105mm, through University Microfilms Inc., 300 North Zeeb Road, Ann Arbor, Michigan 48106.

LC 85-645339   ISSN 0271-0579   ISBN 1-55542-737-5

NEW DIRECTIONS FOR INSTITUTIONAL RESEARCH is part of The Jossey-Bass Higher and Adult Education Series and is published quarterly by Jossey-Bass Inc., Publishers, 350 Sansome Street, San Francisco, California 94104-1310 (publication number USPS 098-830). Second-class postage paid at San Francisco, California, and at additional mailing offices. POST-MASTER: Send address changes to New Directions for Institutional Research, Jossey-Bass Inc., Publishers, 350 Sansome Street, San Francisco, California 94104-1310.

SUBSCRIPTIONS for 1992 cost $45.00 for individuals and $60.00 for institutions, agencies, and libraries.

EDITORIAL CORRESPONDENCE should be sent to the Editor-in-Chief, Patrick T. Terenzini, Center for the Study of Higher Education, The Pennsylvania State University, 403 South Allen Street, Suite 104, University Park, Pennsylvania 16801-5202.

Photograph of the library by Michael Graves at San Juan Capistrano by Chad Slattery © 1984. All rights reserved.

 The paper used in this journal is acid-free and meets the strictest guidelines in the United States for recycled paper (50 percent recycled waste, including 10 percent post-consumer waste). Manufactured in the United States of America.

CONTENTS

EDITORS' NOTES

What is policy analysis? What are the intellectual and theoretical roots for policy analysis? How is it done? How is policy analysis in higher education different from public administration policy analysis? Does policy analysis differ from institutional research? From planning? What contribution can an institutional researcher make to educational policy analysis? What kind of training is needed in order to do policy analysis?

Policy analysis is growing in importance as public and independent higher education institutions plan their futures and address the issues facing them. Limited resources (both financial and personnel), more complex issues, and increasing demands for diverse services contribute to an environment growing ever more complex. Decisions are often made under time pressures and with incomplete information. Policy analysis is a tool for dealing with this complexity and is a way of framing the debate. Educational policy analysis is a systematic blend of analytical and intuitive approaches to understanding the issues, problems, and, most of all, the educational environment. The policy analyst develops an understanding of the issues that can then assist the decision maker in surviving in an increasingly constrained and difficult environment. Well done, policy analysis lays the groundwork for successful policy implementation by field testing the analysis and recommendations with the groups affected by the proposed issue.

Although policy analysis has been taught for many years in graduate schools of business administration, public affairs, and management, its place in the higher education curriculum is more recent. Policy analysis is especially suitable for settings with multiple actors and many interest groups. Policy analysis provides a logic for decision making where balance sheets or profit-and-loss statements do not apply.

Policy-making includes policy formulation, analysis of existing policy, and identification of areas where policy is needed. The policy process becomes a framework within which government action takes place. Boundaries become clearer through the process of policy analysis, policy research, and policy formulation.

As workers in the management and governance of higher education, institutional researchers need to have a coherent view of policy—analysis, policy-making, and policy implementation. Their detailed knowledge of the institutions and the higher education environment is vital to policy analysis. But there are differences between policy analysis and institutional research. Policy analysis aims at gaining as complete a description as possible of the environment, whereas institutional research typically focuses on a subset of environmental factors. Institutional researchers test their work with statistical rigor using methodologies drawn from psychometrics, survey research, and statistics. Policy analysts have to be content with less rigor. Policy analysts use the work of institutional researchers as part of their own work, and their studies may give rise to institutional research studies. Institutional researchers may be asked to write part or all of a policy study or to review a proposed policy for its feasibility. Their studies may suggest areas that need detailed policy review. In some cases, institutional researchers may carry out the implementation of policy recommendations. Institutional researchers often serve as key staff members to the institutional or governing board executive who is involved in setting policy. The work of institutional researchers can be used at several stages in policy development and analysis.

The outcomes of institutional research and policy analysis are also different. Policy analysis deals with the question of what the institution or system should do—goals, directions, and the institutional processes for achieving those goals. In contrast, institutional research focuses on describing and measuring the environment.

This volume, *Developing Effective Policy Analysis in Higher Education*, has three goals: (1) to acquaint the institutional researcher with the field of policy analysis; what it is, where it came from, and how it is carried out; (2) to identify the contributions that institutional research makes to policy analysis in terms of comparative institutional information, methodological rigor, and statistical refinement; and (3) to provide examples of policy analysis studies. In Chapter One, we provide a survey of the literature of policy analysis, organized in the same framework that is developed in Chapter Two, where we lay out a road map of how to do policy analysis. In Chapter Three, Laura Saunders elaborates on the nature of policy analysis by differentiating it from institutional research and planning. With the review of the literature, the description of how to conduct policy analysis, and the clarification of distinctions between institutional research, planning, and policy analysis in these three introductory chapters, the reader is then ready to consider three case studies.

Policy analysis is by its nature messy, grounded in the real world and repetitive. Policymakers often visit and revisit the same issue in only slightly changed forms. Policy analysis is more like sailing than sprinting: The objective is usually clear, but the process of achieving it may require a number of "tacks," back and forth. The three case studies of policy analysis in Chapters Four through Six illustrate these real-world travails.

In Chapter Four, Stephen M. Jordan describes how the University of Arizona approached the policy problem of estimating unmet student demand and locating new institutions. He uses an iterative, repetitive process in revisiting the policy issue.

Sexual harassment cases provide another kind of policy problem—how to understand and develop meaningful procedural policy. In Chapter

Five, Steven G. Olswang describes policy formulation arising out of a case of alleged sexual discrimination by a faculty member against a student at the University of Washington.

In Chapter Six, Roslyn R. Elms discusses the policy issues inherent to meeting the changing and evolving needs of faculty staffing at the University of California, Berkeley. The tasks of hiring and retaining faculty in the face of predicted large-scale retirements provide unique opportunities for a campus to change. By approaching faculty replacement as a comprehensive policy issue, an institution can build a framework for decision making and coherent long-range strategizing.

In Chapter Seven, we analyze these three case studies in terms of the framework developed in Chapter Two, pointing out the key features of policy analysis described in each. Our aim is to demonstrate the complexity of policy analysis.

In Chapter Eight, Kenneth P. Mortimer describes his transformation from policy analyst and institutional researcher to policymaker and university president, reflecting on the nature of policy analysis as seen from the president's chair. He stresses the need for the policy analyst to be continually aware of the institutional context of the decision maker. The pressures of too little time and too much to read constrain any policy analyst's work.

Finally, in Chapter Nine, we provide ideas on how to begin to build the institutional capability to conduct policy analysis and offer a few concluding tips on how to conduct a successful analysis.

> Judith I. Gill
> Laura Saunders
> Editors

JUDITH I. GILL is director of research and policy analysis for the Western Interstate Commission for Higher Education, Boulder, Colorado.

LAURA SAUNDERS is dean of administration at Highline Community College, Des Moines, Washington.

Policy analysis is a real-world decision-making tool. The literature is published, most frequently, in public administration studies, but also in political science, philosophy, organizational psychology, economics, and business administration.

Toward a Definition of Policy Analysis

Judith I. Gill, Laura Saunders

"The Science of Muddling Through" is the title of one of the first and most cited articles on policy analysis (Lindblom, 1959). The title hints at the complexity and messiness of policy analysis. It also gives a clue to the early credibility of policy analysis in academe: limited. Policy analysis does not conform to the traditional rules of good scholarly research.

A Brief History of Policy Analysis

An early version of policy analysis received significant attention in the 1960s. Planning-programming-budgeting-system (PPBS) was introduced by Secretary of Defense Robert McNamara in 1961, and, in 1965, President Johnson issued an executive order requiring its use by all federal agencies. PPBS was instituted to improve budget decision making and to base budget decisions on a cost-benefit analysis of program objectives. However, PPBS did not work because it did not recognize the politics of budget making in its analysis of policy decisions (Weathersby and Balderston, 1972).

The importance of policy analysis in decision making was cited by Congress in the Legislative Reorganization Act of 1970. In this statute, the Congressional Research Service was directed to develop on request "a reasonable approximation of policy analysis," which was defined as a broader, more focused decision analysis that takes into account the nature of the organizations and their environments (Beckman, 1977a). The objective was to make the congressional decision-making process more rational.

The importance of policy analysis as a course of academic study is noted in the development of public administration programs funded, in part, with grants from the Ford Foundation in the early 1970s (Engelbert, 1977). In-

NEW DIRECTIONS FOR INSTITUTIONAL RESEARCH, no. 76, Winter 1992   © Jossey-Bass Publishers

stitutions that received funding included the Graduate School of Public Policy at the University of California in Berkeley, the School of Urban and Public Affairs at Carnegie-Mellon, the John F. Kennedy School of Government at Harvard, the Institute of Public Policy Studies at the University of Michigan, the Lyndon B. Johnson School of Public Affairs at the University of Texas, and the Graduate Institute of the Rand Corporation. The Ford Foundation's interest was to improve the public sector. Its members believed that government agencies needed professionals capable of analysis and management of complex problems.

Most public administration programs offer a master's degree, and, from the beginning, the core subject matter has included the following: "a. quantitative methods, including mathematical programming and modeling, and descriptive and inferential statistics; b. the political and institutional environment of policy formulation and implementation; c. economic theory and analysis emphasizing public-private relationships in resource allocation; d. decision-making and implementation strategies; and e. program management, control, and evaluation" (Engelbert, 1977, p. 230). Moreover, the Rand Corporation is widely known for its studies in the 1960s and 1970s in public policy analysis as well as for its contribution in defining the meaning and use of policy analysis (Ukeles, 1977; Quade, 1975; Coleman, 1972; Straunch, 1974).

What Is Policy Analysis and Why Is It Important?

The traditional academic research approach is not effective in policy analysis because the "research" questions and the framework for investigation are determined by a client's problem, not by a disciplinary interest (Quade, 1975). Policy analysis is not grounded in a strict, discipline-based research methodology because no one discipline is appropriate to reviewing, researching, and analyzing complex policy problems (Lindblom, 1979).

There is no one definition of policy analysis. There is consensus, however, that it is a decision-making tool and that decisions, not actions, are its organizing unit (Lindblom, 1959; Cates, 1979; Dreyfus, 1969; Braybrooke and Lindblom, 1963; Fincher, 1987; Beckman, 1977; Balderston and Weathersby, 1973; Ukeles, 1977; Wildavsky, 1979; Quade, 1975; Stokey and Zeckhauser, 1978; Straunch, 1974; Mushkin, 1977).

Fincher (1987) describes policy analysis as the most effective means available for clarifying policy issues. He highlights its importance in separating complex issues into smaller and more manageable problems for the purposes of interpreting, analyzing, and developing implementation strategies.

Policy analysis is also seen as a method for structuring information and providing opportunities for the development of alternative choices for the policymaker (Balderston and Weathersby, 1973; Beckman, 1977b; Mushkin, 1977; Ukeles, 1977). In the early policy analysis literature, the articulation of alternatives was identified as a key criterion of good policy analysis and the vehicle for providing information on the relative advantages and disadvantages of different policy choices (Wildavsky, 1969; Mushkin, 1977).

Policy analysis can assist in improving the functioning of organizations. Because of goal conflicts within an organization and its environment, analysis is needed to guide informed decision making (Straunch, 1974). Policy analysis provides one source of information and insight for the policymaker. Braybrooke and Lindblom (1963) suggest that policy analysis in the political sector is useful when refining objectives, developing strategies, or setting priorities for policy development. B. Smith (1977, p. 254) provides a somewhat humorous, but reasonably accurate description of policy analysis: "You can tell what policy analysis is by looking at what someone who is not in the government but who is working on public problems is doing. It looks like, but is not, staff work, and it looks like, but is not academic research. It is a mixture of the two called policy analysis."

Policy Analysis Tools

All of the above definitions and approaches suggest that policy analysis is rational and logical. However, there are many who argue otherwise. Cates (1979) suggests that policy analysis is neither rational nor linear but rather draws strongly on intuition and is a messy and elusive creative process. The use of intuition in the policy analysis process also is heralded by Straunch (1974), who believes that policy analysis is used to examine the "squishy" problems, which cannot be represented by mathematical models. Analysis is strongly grounded in the analyst's judgment and intuition of the problem, for solution of nonquantifiable problems demands a role for subjective human judgment. Even in the political science literature, policy analysis is seen as a judgmental process (Straunch, 1974).

In policy analysis, the analyst sometimes must do things that appear to be right but cannot be completely justified or even verified. The process of field-testing ideas and draft analysis can be a means by which the analyst subjects intuition to a real-world check. It can become the built-in "relative" safeguard in a process that can never take into account all relevant values (Lindblom, 1959).

Many writers on policy analysis also call attention to the iterative nature of the process (Quade, 1975; Beckman, 1977a; Lindblom, 1959; Kramer, 1975; Stokey and Zeckhauser, 1978). Instead of disappearing, issues change in response to their exposure and criticism. And, thus, the orderly progression of analysis from one step to another is the exception rather than the rule. "An analyst will [not] always proceed in an orderly fashion from one stage of the analysis to the next. Real people can rarely operate so neatly, nor should they try. The conduct of an analysis will usually turn out in practice to be an iterative process, with the analyst working back and forth among the tasks of identifying problems, defining objectives, enumerating possible alternatives, predicting outcomes, establishing criteria, and valuing trade-off, to reaffirm analysis. This is an entirely sensible approach" (Stokey and Zeckhauser, 1978, p. 6).

Diagnosing the Policy Analysis Problem

The first step in analysis is to define the goals, objectives, and intended outcomes of the analysis (Quade, 1975). What is to be accomplished? What is the underlying problem that requires analysis? What needs to be clarified before going forward? Objectives are what the decision maker seeks to accomplish, and there must be agreement on these objectives. Analysis outcomes that are "off the mark" are usually the result of an analysis that began without clearly understood objectives (Quade, 1975).

A focus on objectives is also useful because it directs attention to the long-term questions of resource availability and options for using those resources (Beckman, 1977b). Fincher (1987) points out that there also can be differences between the stated objectives and the implicit objectives, and the analyst must sort out the steps needed to reach both sets of objectives.

Environment. The literature clearly defines the importance of under-standing the environment when conducting policy analysis (Balderston and Weathersby, 1972; Heydinger, 1985; Katz and Kahn, 1978; Lindblom, 1959; Quade, 1975; Pfeffer and Salancik, 1978; Straunch, 1974; Wildavsky, 1979). Policy analysis must reflect the culture of the problem as well as the more formal elements of organization, decision making, rules, and regulations.

The real-world nature of policy analysis is highlighted by Quade (1975), who states that policy analysis must be appropriate to the environment, the time, and the problem. In the real world, the policymakers' goals and values influence their decisions, and, thus, policy analysis must identify the values, assumptions, and data that influence decision making (Lindblom, 1959; Nagel and Neef, 1978).

The environmental focus suggests a pragmatic approach to policy analysis. Policy analysis is concerned with the effective manipulation of the real world, even if not all of the underlying phenomena are understood (Quade, 1975). While a full description of the environment is desirable, it is probably an elusive goal; there are just too many components for inclusion (Fincher, 1987). The complexities of the real world preclude single-focus analysis as well as any single, best solution. Braybrooke and Lindblom (1963) identify policy analysis as a process of "disjointed incrementalism," a description with which many analysts would agree. Simon (1961) uses the term "bounded rationality" to suggest the same overwhelming task of trying to completely describe the environment. The development of skill in determining what to leave out is part of the training of the analyst and may eventually differentiate good and effective analysis from that which results in poor decision making.

Systems theory helps the analyst by pointing out that organizational relationships are based on interdependent and dependent patterns of interactions (Pfeffer and Salancik, 1978), and these patterns are in a constant state of change. The interdependent nature of organizations contributes to the complexity of the environment, and it is this interdependency that explains the iterative nature of policy analysis.

Boundaries and Constraints. A "rough" analysis of the boundaries of a problem at the beginning helps to focus the investigation. Definition of criteria, terms, and the conceptual framework is an essential starting point (Miles and Huberman, 1984).

While defining the objectives and deciding on the scope of the analysis, the policy analyst, at an early stage, also has to think about the entire problem and decide which aspects to study and which to purposely leave out (Quade, 1975) though the decisions should always remain open to reexamination. The analyst must accept the reality that in policy analysis it is impossible to consider all of the important issues, unless "important" is so narrowly defined that the analysis is in fact quite limited (Lindblom, 1959). Many authors agree that the complexity of the process precludes complete knowledge. Braybrooke and Lindblom (1963) list complexities such as the costs of extended analysis, the absence of a rational system, the open arena in which policy issues are considered, and the diversity of forms that policy can take. Analysts must adjust their own expectations for the completed work to the realities of time and the limitations of the data (Ukeles, 1977).

Balderston and Weathersby (1973) emphasize the constraining factor of time. While good policy analysis takes time, policy decisions frequently must be made quickly, and the analyst has to assess the risks involved in being wrong when policy analysis is conducted within strict time requirements. Coleman (1972) points out that partial information at the right time is better than complete information too late.

Policy analysis is eclectic and draws from a wide range of skills (Beckman, 1977a) and methodologies from disciplines such as history, comparative studies, sociology, political science, and legislative and technological studies. Statistical methodologies such as multiple correlation, log-linear modeling, and analysis of variance provide insights into relationships among variables in the environment.

There are many choices of methodologies that can be used in policy analysis. Wildavsky (1969) suggests the use of political theory for defining the direction of analyses, and quantitative modeling for systematically guessing how to get there. Microeconomic theory provides methodologies for analyzing the use of limited resources, and macrosystems theory offers approaches to correcting systematic error. The choices of hypotheses and research design are determined by the client, the problem, and the environment (Quade, 1975).

Dror (1968) suggests that policy analysis combines proven methods of systems theory with qualitative analysis and an understanding of the policy environment. Quantitative methods include mathematical programming, modeling, and descriptive and inferential statistics. The qualitative methodologies include political and institutional analysis, economic theory, and case studies. Behavioral and nonbehavioral decision making (Engelbert, 1977) assist in the analysis of decision and implementation strategies and processes.

To the frustration of the beginning policy analyst, none of the writers suggests that there is a narrowly defined spectrum of analytical methods. The methods of policy analysis are eclectic, broad, and heuristic and are much looser than the methods used in traditional academic research. A team approach to policy analysis encompassing a variety of disciplines is more apt to be successful than is a focus on a narrow subset of disciplines (Beckman, 1977a).

Models for Unraveling the Policy Analysis Knot

Just as there is no one definition of policy analysis, there is no agreed-on "recipe" for conducting policy analysis (Stokey and Zeckhauser, 1978). The Balderston and Weathersby (1972) model (1) begins with an understanding of the need to make a decision, (2) continues with an identification of the relevant variables, and (3) seeks an understanding of the relationships among the variables that the decision maker controls and the remaining "uncontrolled" relevant variables. The analyst must then (4) examine the values associated with the output or consequences of the decision, (5) evaluate the alternative strategies characterized by the different specifications of the control variables, and, finally, (6) design the decision.

Straunch (1974) divides analysis into the formulation of the formal problem and the mathematical model of the problem. The mathematical analysis of the model determines the logically valid results and the interpretation of the results, both formally and substantively. Balderston and Weathersby (1972) agree with Straunch that when conducting policy analysis, the stages of analysis blur together.

Lindblom's (1959) model is based on his belief that it is impossible to take all important factors into consideration in analysis, and that because policy change does not occur in "leaps and bounds" but rather is incremental, analysis should be grounded in "successive limited comparisons" of information. He argues against the traditional rational-comprehensive model for understanding policy-making because this is not the way policy is made in the real world. An understanding of what is needed comes in incremental and interrelated stages. For example, the value goals and empirical analysis of needed action are not distinct but closely related. Means-ends analysis is not appropriate in policy analysis because the means and ends are not themselves distinct. "Muddling through" generally results in a policy on which various analysts can agree, even if they do not all agree that it is the single best choice for reaching an agreed-on objective. Because the successive comparisons are not done within a strict logical framework, the associated supporting analysis may be somewhat limited. Not all possible outcomes may be included, alternative potential problems are not adequately identified, and some affected values may be overlooked. Successive comparisons also do not rely on a theoretical foundation, as do more formal analysis methods.

Cates (1979) takes issue with Lindblom's model (1959). Her concern with the research tactic of incrementalism and muddling through is based on its limited and conservative nature: "Incrementalism is best-suited to a stable environment where fine-tuning is all that is needed. But what happens when you need to change the channel? Incrementalism is not suited to rapidly changing conditions or to changes in policy direction" (1979, p. 528). Cates's model is based on creativity. The approach is nonrational; the basic strategy is significant advancement; the focus is new not incremental; the criterion for good policy is a restructuring of the problem so that new solutions are found; the techniques for policy analysis include challenging assumptions, brainstorming, and problem solving; and the policy analysis values are intuition, innovation, change, ambiguity, and risk.

Implementation Issues

Students of policy analysis (for example, Quade, 1975; Coleman, 1972; Beckman, 1977a, 1977b; and Schick, 1977) have addressed the question of how policy can be implemented, and the way in which implementation issues affect policy analysis and decisions. Quade (1975) reinforces the position that success in policy analysis requires that the analyst attempt to understand how the policy being investigated is and will be constrained by the institutions and individuals affected by the proposed policy. Good analysis identifies these constituency groups and the factors that may help to ensure the acceptance of policy. Analysis of the implementation effects of policy requires that the analyst develop models that take into account secondary and tertiary effects. Good policy analysis requires prediction of consequences.

Coleman (1972) distinguishes policy outcomes as intended and unintended and suggests that both deserve examination. The voices of those individuals who are unintentionally affected by policy may substantially affect policy implementation. Beckman (1977a, 1977b) suggests that good policy analysis should contribute to the process of clarifying alternative policies and their implications.

There is agreement that policy is not made once and for all time; rather, it is made and remade endlessly. Policy-making is a process of successive approximation to a changing objective. Policy-making does not proceed in a straight line to a single, agreed-on, and unchanging objective. At best, policy-making is a rough process. In this more general context, Cates (1979) indicates that creativity plays an essential role and may be a more appropriate description of the process than is "muddling through."

Policy Analysis in Higher Education

A comprehensive understanding of the environment is a key to good policy analysis, because policy analysis is about real-world problems and real-world decisions. Good analysis depends on the analyst's understanding of the setting and the actors. Analytical models appropriate in some environments may not be appropriate to the environments of higher education.

Balderston and Weathersby (1972) point out a number of crucial higher education characteristics that can affect analysis. Educational institutions foster diversity rather than promote uniformity; they seek differentiated instead of homogeneous viewpoints. Colleges and universities have decentralized management with hundreds of largely interdependent decision makers, and decisions are not top-down but rather collegial in nature. A unified institutionwide mission and objectives are the exception rather than the rule in higher education. Colleges and universities also deal with larger clienteles beyond their immediate boundaries. Alumni, the surrounding communities, state systems, governing structures, legislators, donors, and business and industry affect higher education and are affected by it.

Actions in one arena have effects in quite different arenas in ways that may be only dimly understood in the process of policy formulation. Particularly in public higher education institutions, but also to a considerable extent in the independent sector, this external political context circumscribes the scope of acceptable decisions, but it does not preclude creativity in decision making.

References

Balderston, F. E., and Weathersby, G. B. "PPBS in Higher Education Planning and Management: Part II, The University of California Experience." *Higher Education: An International Journal of Higher Education and Educational Planning,* 1972, 1 (3), 299–319.

Balderston, F. E., and Weathersby, G. B. "PPBS in Higher Education Planning and Management: Part III, Perspectives and Applications of Policy Analysis." *Higher Education: An International Journal of Higher Education and Educational Planning,* 1973, 2 (1), 33–67.

Beckman, N. "Policy Analysis for the Congress." *Public Administration Review,* 1977a, 37 (3), 237–244.

Beckman, N. "Policy Analysis in Government: Alternatives to Muddling Through." *Public Administration Review,* 1977b, 37 (3), 221–222.

Braybrooke, D., and Lindblom, C. E. *A Strategy of Decision: Policy Evaluation as a Social Process.* New York: Free Press, 1963.

Cates, C. "Beyond Muddling: Creativity." *Public Administration Review,* 1979, 39 (6), 527–532.

Coleman, J. S. *Policy Research in the Social Sciences.* Morristown, N.J.: General Learning Press, 1972.

Dreyfus, D. A. "The Limitations of Policy Research in Congressional Decision Making." *Policy Studies Journal,* 1969, 4 (3), 269.

Dror, Y. *Public Policymaking Reexamined.* San Francisco: Chandler, 1968.

Engelbert, E. A. "University Education for Public Policy Analysis." *Public Administration Review,* 1977, 37 (3), 228–236.

Fincher, C. "Policy Analysis and Institutional Research." In M. W. Peterson and L. A. Mets (eds.),

Key Resources on Higher Education Governance, Management, and Leadership: A Guide to the Literature. San Francisco: Jossey-Bass, 1987.

Heydinger, R. B. "Forces Affecting the Future of Postsecondary Education." In M. W. Peterson and M. Corcoran (eds.), *Institutional Research in Transition.* New Directions for Institutional Research, no. 46. San Francisco: Jossey-Bass, 1985.

Katz, D., and Kahn, R. L. *The Social Psychology of Organizations.* New York: Wiley, 1978.

Kramer, F. A. "Policy Analysis as Ideology." *Public Administration Review,* 1975, 35 (5), 509–517.

Lindblom, C. E. "The Science of Muddling Through." *American Economic Review,* 1959, 48, 313–328.

Lindblom, C. E. "Still Muddling, Not Yet Through." *Public Administration Review,* 1979, 39 (6), 517–526.

Miles, M. B., and Huberman, A. M. *Qualitative Data Analysis: A Sourcebook of New Methods.* Newbury Park, Calif.: Sage, 1984.

Mushkin, S. J. "Policy Analysis in State and Community." *Public Administration Review,* 1977, 37 (3), 245–253.

Nagel, S., and Neef, M. "Finding an Optimum Choice Level, or Mix, in Policy Analysis." *Public Administration Review,* 1978, 38 (5), 404–412.

Pfeffer, J., and Salancik, G. R. *The External Control of Organizations: A Resource Dependence Perspective.* New York: HarperCollins, 1978.

Quade, E. S. *Analysis for Public Decisions.* New York: Elsevier Science, 1975.

Schick, A. "Beyond Analysis." *Public Administration Review,* 1977, 37 (3), 258–263.

Simon, H. A. *Administrative Behavior.* New York: Macmillan, 1961.

Smith, B.L.R. "The Non-Governmental Policy Analysis Organization." *Public Administration Review,* 1977, 37 (3), 253–258.

Stokey, E., and Zeckhauser, R. *A Primer for Policy Analysis.* New York: Norton, 1978.

Straunch, R. E. *A Critical Assessment of Quantitative Methodology as a Policy Analysis Tool.* Santa Monica, Calif.: Rand Corporation, 1974.

Ukeles, J. B. "Policy Analysis: Myth or Reality?" *Public Administration Review,* 1977, 37 (3), 223–228.

Weathersby, G. B., and Balderston, F. E. "PPBS in Higher Education Planning and Management: Part I, An Overview." *Higher Education: An International Journal of Higher Education and Educational Planning,* 1972, 1 (2), 191–206.

Wildavsky, A. "Rescuing Policy Analysis from PPBS." *Public Administration Review,* 1969, 34 (2), 189–202.

Wildavsky, A. *Speaking Truth to Power: The Art and Craft of Policy Analysis.* Boston: Little, Brown, 1979.

JUDITH I. GILL is director of research and policy analysis for the Western Interstate Commission for Higher Education, Boulder, Colorado.

LAURA SAUNDERS is dean of administration at Highline Community College, Des Moines, Washington.

What does an institutional researcher do when assigned a policy analysis?

Conducting Policy Analysis in Higher Education

Judith I. Gill, Laura Saunders

Policy analysis is a real-world phenomenon and, as such, is subject to all of the ambiguity characteristic of real-world problems and issues. Policy analysis describes a type of applied research and analysis conducted for policymakers to assist them in the decision-making process. Policy analysis is broader than an analysis of a policy issue, or development of a policy statement. It can include an analysis of the impact of an existing policy, or an analysis of activities having a direct or indirect relationship to policy. For example, it can include an analysis of issues affecting enrollment policies, student rights issues, or issues influencing faculty hiring and promotion decisions.

Policy analysis in higher education requires an understanding of the issues, but, equally important, it requires an understanding of the higher education environment, including interrelationships of forces and structures within the environment. Any attempt to develop recommendations on faculty hiring, as Elms (this volume) explains, is meaningless without an understanding of the role of departments and colleges.

Policy analysis is not a discrete, self-contained activity. It is a process involving continuous review and evaluation of new information against existing information. It is a process that is sensitive to organizational culture and politics, and that continuously scans the environment looking for

Note: The authors would like to acknowledge the assistance of Dr. Ellen Wagner, professor of education, Northern Colorado University, for her assistance in developing Figure 2.1, Conducting Policy Analysis in Higher Education.

important interactions among people, resources, and organizations. It also requires a focused examination of factors affecting policy implementation. Policy analysis is a fascinating process, and because limited fiscal resources require tough decision making involving interdependent activities, it is critical to the development and maintenance of a quality system of higher education.

In this chapter, we lay out a road map for the policy analyst. However, the analyst's path is unlikely to be a straight line from beginning to end. Try to visualize a length of helix coil: The issues in the analysis are strung out along a spiral that cuts through a variety of environmental and structural issues, and many issues will be examined more than once in the course of the analysis. The road map for conducting policy analysis in higher education is diagrammed in Figure 2.1. The repetitive nature of policy analysis is highlighted by the interrelationships among the policy analysis stages, policy analysis tools and the outputs of analysis.

Figure 2.1. Conducting
Policy Analysis in Higher Education

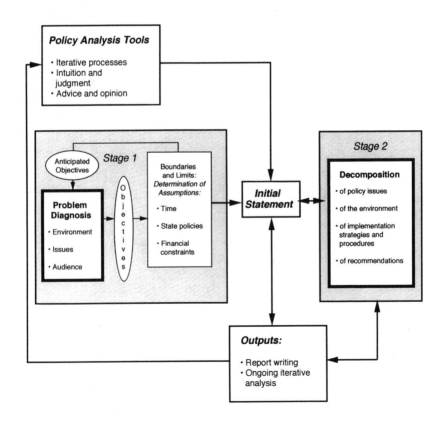

Policy Analysis Tools

The policy analyst uses three basic tools: the iterative process, intuition and judgment, and the advice and opinions of others. The iterative process is a requirement because most decisions, especially those important enough to require policy analysis, will affect other policies and practices. This spillover effect is widespread in higher education because colleges and universities have interdependent relationships with their environments; they do not exist as closed systems.

The iterative process of constant examination and reexamination may be frustrating and, to some, may appear redundant. However, if a combination of common sense and intuition are used to ensure that the objectives of the analysis are maintained and that the boundaries remain realistic, the iterative process ensures good analysis; and good analysis is analysis that can be used because it has been developed by continuous measurement against real-world factors.

While the rational higher education environment does not easily admit to the role of intuition in analysis, it is an important tool. Policy analysis requires an accurate reading of the politics of the organization and its people, and this is based as much on intuition as it is on rational and logical analysis of an issue. Intuition is honed by years of experience in the organization and an understanding of and sensitivity to the forces that affect change. Recommendations that are a logical outcome of good analysis, but deficient in the understanding of politics, will miss the mark. Mortimer (this volume) provides two excellent policy analysis examples that were analytically correct but politically wrong and thus significantly flawed.

Finally, the true test of policy analysis is in the real world, and the policy analyst is rare who has or who can gain, in isolation, a comprehensive understanding of all of the issues that should be considered. Therefore, field testing is an important analytical tool. There are several approaches that can be taken to field testing, but one of the more useful is to identify a panel of advisers and use these individuals to discuss the analysis as it proceeds.

Unlike an objective fact-finding panel, the policy analyst wants advisers who have vested interests or even biases in the policy area. Unbiased reactors do not provide crucial information on acceptability and implementation in the real world. This field-testing group should have a commitment to the issue and some area of expertise that expands the analyst's understanding.

Advisers are an invaluable source of information. They can save the analyst substantial time in researching the issues. They serve as reactors to the analytical work throughout its course. The sense of the experienced institutional observer or politician as to what will or will not work in a particular setting can save the analyst from embarrassing misstatements.

Field testing is conducted when there is new information to be examined, when there are significant changes in the environment, and when models and recommendations are being discussed. Field testing eliminates some of the surprises that frequently accompany the announcement of recommendations, surprises that may impede or kill the adoption of recommendations.

There are risks to field testing. Because the advisers have vested interests, they may lobby the analyst into a position that clouds objectivity. However, the benefits of an advisory panel outweigh the costs because the failure to consult with others limits the opportunity for comprehensive understanding of the issues.

How to Do Policy Analysis

Writing about "how to do policy analysis" is difficult because the process is not linear; each step does not follow from the previous one. The following description of "how to do" is grouped by general features, but the order may vary in any given analysis.

There are two major stages of analysis. The first is a mini-analysis of the problem to be investigated. It requires an identification of the study's objectives, environment, and limitations. It concludes with the development of an initial statement of analysis. This statement is the foundation for the second stage of analysis where many interdependent components of the issue are investigated and recommendations tied to the objectives of the analysis are constructed.

Stage 1: Diagnosing the Problem. The policy analyst's work begins with a preliminary sketch or initial statement of the issues and factors to be included in the analysis. The statement may best be understood by thinking of it as the strategy for analysis. It should be written, because the writing process is an analytical tool. If possible, it also should be reviewed and approved by the person making the assignment; this usually is the policymaker who will use the analysis. Jordan (this volume) provides a good example of an initial statement of analysis that guided the enrollment planning analysis used by the Arizona University System.

Because university life and activities within its environment do not stop while analysis is conducted, the initial statement may require modification as work progresses. For example, Olswang (this volume) explains how the University of Washington's initial strategy for investigating a sexual harassment complaint was changed because of a newspaper advertisement.

Most analysts expect continuous modification of their analysis strategies. Unlike a controlled laboratory experiment with a predetermined protocol, policy analysis is analogous to investigatory laboratory work. The analyst starts with a general idea of what to expect and how to proceed but is open to new ideas that are formulated as data are collected and analyzed.

The policy analyst who is inflexible and unwilling to make changes to the initial strategy may end up with recommendations that are not useful because they are not applicable to an environment that changed while the analysis was being conducted. If the recommendations do not reflect new information as well as the changed environment, they may not be adopted. As in legal cases, the analysis may become moot.

Defining the Objectives. There are two kinds of objectives that must be understood and accounted for in the analysis: the assigned objective of the study and the objective of the policymaker. There may be several objectives within each category, and there may be conflicts among the objectives.

The analyst begins by clarifying the study's objectives. Answers to very basic questions are needed: Why should the analysis be conducted? And what are the intended outcomes of this analysis? The objectives are the reasons for conducting the analysis. They can include policy clarification, evaluation of the impact of policy, or identification and analysis of practices that have an impact on policy. The intended outcome of the analysis may be a recommendation for policy revision, adoption of new campus practices and procedures, or development of a model to predict certain outcomes based on given policies or environmental conditions.

In 1990, the Western Interstate Commission for Higher Education (WICHE) began an analysis of the relationship between higher education and the economy, the objective of which was to help state policymakers understand this relationship so that higher education's role in improving the state's economy would be considered during the budget development process. The intended outcomes of the study were policy recommendations promoting a strengthening of this relationship (Western Interstate Commission for Higher Education, 1992).

Higher education policy analysis is most frequently conducted to assist in the decision-making process of policymakers such as a university administrator, a governing board member, or a legislator. Therefore, the policymaker's objectives must be understood. However, the assigned objective of the analysis may not always be the policymaker's objective. For example, the objective of the analysis may be to demonstrate institutional accountability to a state higher education coordinating board, and the desired outcome may be no change in current campus practices and policies. The analyst needs to understand these circumstances and prepare accordingly. The naive analyst may arrive at loggerheads with institutional leaders if the objective is not understood and taken into account in the preparation of the analysis. Unless the real objective is understood, many hours of analytical effort may be spent in areas that do not meet the policymaker's objectives.

In the problem diagnosis stage, possible conflicts among objectives may also be identified. The objectives may inherently conflict with the interests of important constituencies as well as produce tension between the analyst and the policymaker. These conflicts in objectives need to be identified early in the analytical process so that they can be resolved or so that factors related to areas of conflict can be addressed as part of the analysis.

A final word about defining the objectives of analysis: The analyst must not expect the objectives to remain static and unchanging. The objectives of analysis, as well as the intended outcomes, may change over the course of the investigation as more information is learned, better data are gathered and examined, and a more complete understanding of the underlying factors is gained. Stubborn adherence to the original definition of the objectives may limit the analysis unduly and preclude a full examination of the issues.

Understanding the Environment. Policy analysis requires a comprehensive understanding of the environment and culture affected by the policy being examined. This includes an understanding of the organization's values, important current and historical issues, and the organizational structures and decision-making processes.

The environment makes higher education policy analysis different from public policy analysis focusing on federal, state, and local government issues. The higher education environment is dominated by a culture that includes faculty governance, autonomy, and academic freedom; the values of teaching, research, and public service; and, at public colleges and universities, accountability issues.

A basic list of environmental factors includes key individuals who are currently identified with the issue or who may become involved (for example, institutional administrators, staff, faculty, students, governing board members, community leaders, and elected officials) and the responsibilities and influence of these individuals in the operation and decision-making structure of the organization. An understanding of past organizational struggles of a similar nature may help in identifying these individuals.

Identification of important factors provides clues to the location of studies that may prove beneficial to the analysis. Institutional histories and discussions with other analysts who have studied similar issues may provide meaningful insights.

The higher education policy analysis environment includes everything and everyone that has an interdependent relationship with issues being analyzed. But time and resources limit the number of factors that can be included in the analysis. Therefore, the analyst has to identify those factors having the greatest influence on the issue.

The analyst understands that just as the objectives may change over the course of the study, so too does the environment. To adapt a term from computer science, policy analysis is conducted in "real" time, and the world of the institutional executive or state official does not stop while the analyst works. It is imperative that the analyst keep abreast of changes in the environment while work is in progress so that when the analysis is completed, the result fits the real world. For example, recommendations for tuition increases based on an analysis of the relationship between tuition and access policies that did not consider recent action to reduce student loan program funds would be unrealistic.

Boundaries and Limits. Identification of the assumptions that guide analysis is an important component in the diagnosis of the problem. Assumptions provide boundaries for analysis and are factors accepted as truth. Four primary assumptions guided WICHE's analysis of the relationship of higher education to the economy: (1) Higher education's role in the economy is far more comprehensive than is its contribution to economic development. Through teaching, research, and public service, higher education's role involves a wide range of activities from improving the quality of life to promoting economic growth. (2) State policies can serve to strengthen the relationship between higher education and the economy. (3) Financial constraints, in large part, will determine the feasibility of implementing policy recommendations. (4) Because of financial constraints, new models of cooperation and better differentiation among colleges and universities may be needed if higher education is to contribute more effectively to society and to the economy.

Boundaries also are provided by the seriousness of the issue, the environment, and the social forces at play. Policy analysis in a crisis is somewhat different, at least in degree, from policy analysis undertaken in a calm and dispassionate environment. For example, for many colleges and universities, the analysis of divestiture of institutional holdings in South African stocks needed to be done quickly, had significant implications for the institution's credibility with students and other constituent groups, and carried significant financial consequences. The urgency of the issue gave a far different feeling to the policy analysis than would have a long-range financial plan of desired investment yields.

The methodology used in analysis also provides a significant boundary, and it should be identified in the initial statement. It should include not only a brief description of the quantitative and qualitative approaches to be used but also an identification of who and/or what will be consulted for data, opinions, institutional history, and comparative information.

In the course of analysis, the boundaries of an issue almost always expand; therefore, it is important that the initial diagnosis be focused, and that the impact of time and resource limitations on the analysis be identified. Boundaries frequently are determined by the amount of time that can be devoted to the analysis. Deadlines are boundaries that have a particularly formative effect on policy analysis. Frequently, policy analysis work is time-dependent. Rough and timely, rather than exhaustively complete, are the watchwords of the policy analyst.

Initial Statement. The initial statement is the diagnosis of the issue. It identifies the objectives of the analysis, including intended outcomes, important environment factors, and the initial boundaries for analysis that will guide data collection and other research activities. The initial statement also defines the strategy for analysis. It may include the language of the initial request for analysis. It is, however, a far more comprehensive statement. It is the guidepost used throughout the process to judge whether the developing analysis is meeting its objectives.

The write-up of the initial statement provides the opportunity to identify clearly the problems, ambiguities, conflicts, scope, and resource costs. A written statement can serve as the document of agreement between the analyst and the person who made the assignment. Discussion of the written statement can highlight disagreements about or misunderstandings of terms and language.

Terms must be defined and agreed on. Assumed definitions, like assumed values, can be mine fields for the unwary analyst. "I didn't know that was what you meant by retention!" can be the death knell for a substantial piece of work. Language is the tool of the policy analyst, and nowhere is its care and precision more needed than in the initial statement.

Stage 2: Unraveling the Policy Analysis Knot. The initial statement is the analyst's framework for conducting policy analysis, and the analyst will continually refer back to this statement when examining new information.

Four Basic Components. The primary components of policy analysis are the policy issue, the environment, the factors affecting policy implementation, and the proposed alternatives or recommendations. The attention given to each component depends on its relative emphasis in the initial statement of analysis, as well as its importance in the analyst's growing understanding of the issue. If the initiative for policy analysis is a recommendation for developing assessment outcomes, the focus will be on understanding assessment issues. If the initiative is politically motivated, considerable attention will be focused on the environment promoting political concerns. If faculty behavior is being studied, the analysis may emphasize factors affecting the implementation of faculty policies. If the legislature is demanding change, the focus will be on the development of recommendations for new policies.

Of the four components, an understanding of the policy issue is typically the most straightforward. Information may come from available data sources, literature reviews, and surveys that the analyst designs and conducts. An understanding of the environment, identification of factors affecting policy implementation, and development of recommendations or models are more cumbersome. These components require comprehensive knowledge of the organizational structure, its decision-making mode, its information networks, its culture and history, and its people and resources. As well as the individual elements, the analyst also must consider the interrelationships among these factors.

Complex interrelationships are involved in most policy analysis work. The following examples of policy questions illustrate this complexity. First, how will state revenue declines affect the recommendation for a small business development center at a land grant university? Long-range and short-term state and university needs must be examined. Although the center may contribute to state economic development, revenue declines may mean that it only can be funded at the expense of some other project. The federal government will support some of the program costs, thus bringing new dollars into the state, but these dollars will be lost if the state cannot provide its share of needed dollars. Extension programs are an important component of the land grant university's role and mission, and in the twenty-first century the definition of extension should include small business development centers.

Second, how do faculty tenure and promotion policies affect the board of trustees requirement that the college give more attention to teaching? Most tenure and promotion decisions are made by faculty committees in the discipline, and research, not teaching, is the valued activity. Standard criteria exist for evaluating outstanding research. What are the criteria for evaluating outstanding teaching? The outstanding teacher is not the highly sought out faculty member, the outstanding researcher is. External funding is available for research activities, not teaching.

Third, how do accreditation requirements affect the development of telecommunications programs in the health sciences? The health sciences have very strong professional standards and accreditation associations. Many courses offered via telecommunications cannot be evaluated by the same standards as applied to traditionally offered courses. Most professional accreditation associations are dominated by faculty members. The number of faculty members who endorse the offering of telecommunications courses is limited, as is the number who have actually used telecommunications.

A policy analyst's greatest asset is his or her understanding of the higher education environment, and of the many different avenues that need to be explored to determine the potential impact of decisions on institutional policies and practices. However, most policy analysts are generalists, and they should not be expected to understand all of the details of complex problems. Their role is to know where to begin, how to develop the analysis, and how to wrap it up. A detailed understanding of issues can come from other resources and people.

Policy Issue. The process of gaining an understanding of the policy issue is frequently identified in the literature as policy research. Information on policy issues may come from literature reviews, a network of colleagues, campus surveys and data bases, and campus faculty. A literature review frequently provides useful initial insights and may identify methodological frameworks that can be used to array important factors. Examination of existing reviews of the literature (such as those produced in the ASHE-ERIC series), or recent topical articles such as those found in the New Directions for Institutional Research series, can help to identify critical factors. Colleagues can provide information on the development and implementation of similar issues on other campuses. And reviews of available data bases can provide clues to what information is known and what additional information may need to be collected.

Analytical tools are used throughout the investigation to gain a better understanding of the issue. The policy analyst should have a fairly broad acquaintance with the social science research literature since frameworks from a variety of disciplines can be helpful in identifying relevant factors. For example, economic factors are important in understanding issues related to student enrollment trends, while knowledge of small group behavior and organizations may be more helpful in looking at alternative organizational forms for faculty governance.

The seasoned analyst also knows that many higher education issues are recycled issues; not only do they reflect trends in the larger society that are cyclical in nature, but they reflect institutional dynamics of birth, growth and maturity, and decline. Issues related to economic factors are among the most common. The recessions of the mid-1970s and early 1990s brought to institutional attention many of the same issues: balancing of demand and resource constraints, quality and access, and faculty productivity. The fact that so many higher education issues are recycled highlights the importance of understanding their histories of analysis and policy implementation. Incorporation of the results of earlier studies ensures continuity and provides a more comprehensive overview of an issue.

Environment. In stage 1, diagnosing the problem, the analyst identifies the broad array of environmental factors important to the analysis. These factors include people and organizations; policies, practices, and laws; and histories, values, and trends. In stage 2, the interdependency of these factors is fully examined, and as greater understanding of these factors develops, the list may grow.

In assessing the policy environment, the policy analyst assumes the role of institutional politician and gives attention to significant groups within the college or university, as well as to groups external to the institution. Different groups have different interests in policy. Some policies may be of interest to a large number of groups, and others may affect only a small number of people. Understanding the formal and informal authority and prestige structure within an institution is important to understanding the connections among factors.

The analyst must understand the factors that will constrain the implementation of policies and practices and therefore limit the kinds of decisions that can be made. Constraints may be legal: state statutes, administrative procedures, or riders to appropriations acts. Or they may be matters of political and social custom. In the latter case, constraints are sometimes qualified: they may be more or less of a constraint depending on other factors. For example, funding for faculty merit increases may depend on the amount of dollars that are left in the salary pool after allocating cost-of-living increases for all faculty. Political constraints can be internal to the institutions and related to people or culture (for example, involvement of the faculty senate president at meetings of the board of trustees), or external and related to the roles or personalities of governing boards members, state legislators, other college or university administrators, or the general public (for example, unofficial presentation of the university budget request to the higher education coordinating board before it is formally submitted to the governor).

An understanding of the environment is the key to good analysis, and because higher education is a unique organization, the analyst must have a comprehensive understanding of the traditions, values, purposes, and operations of colleges and universities. One of the unique components of higher education as an organization is that although colleges and universities are formally organized along hierarchical lines, there are significant players who do not fit in a neat linear organizational chart and have no formal role in the decision-making process. If recommendations are developed without taking account of significant groups (such as members of the faculty or the student senate), they will have little or no chance of being successfully implemented. It makes no difference that some of these groups do not show up as a box on an organizational chart.

The environmental factors provide clues to the level and type of data and analysis that are needed and appropriate. Recently, several reports were released proclaiming a significant faculty shortage in the late 1990s. Many of these studies based their conclusions on nationally aggregated data. While these reports provided important information, their conclusions were not appropriate to individual colleges and universities. Higher education policy analysts know that institutional decisions related to future faculty supply and demand require institutional data on faculty retirement rates, faculty separation rates and reasons for faculty attrition, student enrollment trends and projections by college, national trends in the number of Ph.D. recipients, and national and local nonacademic employment markets for Ph.D. recipients. Some of these data are hard to collect, for example, national employment markets for Ph.D. recipients, and some of these data may be sensitive, for example, reasons for faculty attrition. Higher education policy analysts also know that if the state coordinating board and/or legislature wants a general idea of the state's faculty supply and demand picture, the required data collection activities will depend on the use of common definitions by colleges and universities. Development of common definitions will be institutionally sensitive.

Implementation and Recommendations. Intended outcomes of analysis are usually recommendations for policy changes, new policies, new practices and procedures, or models that provide a better understanding of the consequences of policy actions. While policy analysis usually does not include implementation activities, a comprehensive analysis needs to consider the factors affecting the implementation of the recommendations.

Intuition, field testing, and the iterative process of analysis provide significant clues to the likelihood of recommendations being implemented. From these policy analysis tools comes the ability to develop realistic recommendations. However, if time permits, the best approach to developing realistic recommendations is to discuss preliminary recommendations with individuals who will have a role in the implementation of "the real thing." The practice of trying out an idea on experienced players can eliminate the initially attractive but infeasible proposal. Presidents and chancellors may have a limited number of issues that they will champion at any one time. Effective presidents develop a strategic sense of what will and will not work on any policy issue.

In developing recommendations for the WICHE project on higher education and the economy, staff analysts discussed with state and higher education policymakers implementation issues relating to draft recommendations calling for greater campus accountability in the use of state funds. While state leaders supported the recommendations, campus leaders indicated frustration with the continual call for accountability in the wise use of state funds which are insufficient for meeting the state's demands. These conversations led to revisions in the recommendations.

The recommendations finally presented to the WICHE commissioners called for the adoption of a state strategic agenda for higher education that identifies both the funding needed for meeting state priority needs and the campus that will meet each need. Campuses are to be held accountable for meeting the specific needs that have been identified and funded. The revised recommendations were adopted.

Initial recommendations or models should be refined and revised after reviewing implementation possibilities. For each recommendation, the analyst must ask, Can it work? Is it likely? Is it reasonable? The goal is to develop the "win-win" recommendation. But policy changes often engender conflict. Given a relatively short time frame and a constrained and politicized environment, the win-win outcome may simply not be possible. In these cases, the analyst should consider discussing the results and recommendations of the analysis with groups that will be negatively affected by the proposed policy, prior to submitting the analysis. Except in political campaigns, the doctrine of no-surprises is almost always a good strategy to adopt and may enable, through minor revisions, the development of "win-almost win" outcomes.

The development of recommendations is shaped by everything that has gone before. The checklist for the final draft of recommendations should include answers to the following questions: Are the objectives addressed? Can they be implemented? Have constraints been addressed?

While policy analysis depends on and draws from research studies, the standards for developing alternatives and recommendations come more from the political arena than the methodological and quantitative arena. However, this does not preclude development of creative recommendations.

Recommendations and models that have been tried in other institutional settings should be included in the final report. Well-publicized solutions adopted at prominent institutions provide reference points for the decision maker and the analyst.

Written Report

The development of recommendations is not the final stage of analysis. The writing process involves considerable analysis in itself. Because writing is an analytical tool, the analyst should not avoid writing until all of the variables are accounted for and the recommendations developed.

The analyst presents the work in a final written report. In addition to brief reviews of the literature and environmental and other factors influencing the study, the main body of the written report focuses on the recommendations and the implementation issues, including, as mentioned above, examples from other states or colleges and universities. A rationale is needed for each recommendation, but the methodology used in the analysis should be very brief or included in an appendix. As a rule, a policy analyst cannot expect the policymaker to read a detailed report. Therefore, the most salient issues must be presented concisely. The analyst must also remember the audiences for the report and provide information in a format and language appropriate to them.

Reference

Western Interstate Commission for Higher Education (WICHE). *Meeting Economic and Social Challenges: A Strategic Agenda for Higher Education (Policy Recommendations)*. Boulder, Colo.: WICHE, 1992.

JUDITH I. GILL is director of research and policy analysis for the Western Interstate Commission for Higher Education.

LAURA SAUNDERS is dean of administration at Highline Community College, Des Moines, Washington.

*Institutional researchers and planners inform policy analysis through
their data analyses, methodologies, and comparative institutional data.*

Policy Analysis: Neither Institutional Research nor Planning

Laura Saunders

Policy analysis is applied research and analysis conducted for policymakers
to assist in the policy decision process. While there is overlap between
institutional research, planning, and policy analysis, they are different. This
chapter discusses the differences and similarities. Several volumes in the
Jossey-Bass series New Directions for Institutional Research (NDIR) are
examined to illustrate the differences. NDIR provides good examples of
policy analysis as well as solid methodological guidance and information
about data sources for the policy analyst.

Institutional Research Versus Policy Analysis

Institutional research has had a variety of definitions over the years and
slowly seems to be coming together as a profession. Joe Saupe (1981, p. 1)
defined institutional research as "research conducted within an institution
of higher education in order to provide information which supports institutional planning, policy formulation, and decision making." An elaboration
of this definition is given in the introduction to the Association for Institutional Research (AIR) publication *A Primer on Institutional Research* (Muffo
and McLaughlin, 1987, p. iv): "processes and functions which can be, and
are, performed in and on most functional areas of the institutions." Thus,
institutional researchers are characterized by where they function—institutions and systems of higher education—and what they do.

These definitions are misleading, however, since institutional research
in recent years has spread beyond a focus on institutions of higher education.
The content of the papers presented at the annual meeting of AIR suggests

the eclectic nature of the profession, with presentation topics including alumni research, outcomes assessment, ranking polls, graduation rates of athletes, and appropriate computer techniques. While traditional colleges and universities and state higher education systems remain a major focus of institutional researchers, vocational and technical schools, proprietary institutions, and national education policy also receive attention.

Institutional research emphasizes data and information: collection, analysis, appropriate methodologies, sources, and uses. This emphasis is particularly important to the policy analyst who frequently calls upon institutional research skills when examining a policy analysis problem. The sourcebooks and meetings of institutional researchers provide a wealth of information on appropriate data sources, the wit and wisdom of making comparisons of various kinds, techniques to find information in masses of data, and even the right questions to ask. Because of their central position as data managers in institutions, systems offices, and agencies, institutional researchers can often identify sources of data or information and may know of previous work that has been done related to the issue under review. In early stages of policy analysis development, the institutional researcher's perspective may help to define the study's objectives and its boundaries. The institutional researcher will always be a strong member of the field-testing group.

Another area where the institutional researcher can make a contribution is in providing a road map to external institutional information sources. Institutional researchers, through their participation in regional and national meetings, connections to electronic networks, and constant review of publications, may be able to identify external sources of data, policy work, or methodologies. Many institutional research offices have access to the burgeoning number of electronic newsletters and lists that are sources of up-to-date information, as well as access to other institutions and settings. Questions are asked and answered, papers sent, and people identified for detailed discussion. The question "Does anybody know anybody who has done anything recently on . . . ?" is a frequent query on the electronic networks, and because of the speed and ease of communication, they are a first-rate resource that the institutional researcher can share with the policy analyst.

Methodologies and appropriate data-handling techniques are the special expertise of the institutional researcher. Policy analysis may require data or information to test alternatives, describe problems, or select recommendations. In particular, institutional researchers can test data for statistical reliability so that policy analysts do not draw invalid inferences from their data. The skillful caution of the institutional researcher is useful to the policy analyst, who often works in a pressured and rushed atmosphere. Jumping to unwarranted conclusions based on incorrect use of data can be very costly to the credibility of the policy analyst. The practice of having the resident institutional researcher review data for validity and reliability may cause a momentary delay, but it can save a policy analyst from mistakes with long-run implications.

There is a delicate balance in the relationship between the data handler (institutional researcher) and the policy analyst. Too much caution may mean that policy work is sometimes not timely, too little may mean that the work is not valid. Typically, however, policy analysts cannot afford to leave the data and research experts out of their consultations.

Besides advice and input on data and methodologies, the institutional researcher is often useful in the initial formulation stages of a project, when the policy analyst is attempting to understand the dimensions of the problem. Because institutional researchers are often involved in a variety of campus projects, they may have unique insights into the institutional climate and environment. In addition, institutional researchers frequently function as local historians and have insights on what has and has not worked, which powerful or influential groups play an active role in the development and dissemination of policy, and which pitfalls exist for the unwary policymaker.

The distinctions, therefore, between institutional research and policy analysis are several: Institutional research focuses on data and information in institutions and systems, whereas policy analysis extends beyond data collection and analysis and makes use of many qualitative research methodologies as well as generous helpings of intuition. Institutional research usually does not point to recommendations or changes, while policy analysis almost always does. The reasons for doing policy analysis reflect real-world issues and the analysis has definite time constraints. Policy analysis takes place in an atmosphere where judgments and biases have already constrained the analysis. Institutional research may require the maintenance of long-term data bases and the production of periodic reports using agreed-on formats. Policy analysis has widely diverse outputs, may draw on a variety of sources of information, including institutional research data bases, and extends beyond the use of quantitative data. Policy analysis frequently includes recommendations for action or reinforcement of existing policies and strategies for implementation; these elements are usually not part of the institutional research agenda. Policy analysts may field-test and revise their recommendations a number of times, while the products of institutional researchers are reports written as of particular points in time. The policy analyst's work is messy, inexact, and grounded in the real world of trying to get things done. Political factors enter into the shaping of the policy analysis and the associated recommendations, while the institutional researcher's work is conducted more independently of political factors. The institutional researcher may often perform policy analysis, and the policy analyst may draw on the work of the institutional researcher, but these actions do not entail the same function.

How does the work of the policy analyst influence that of the institutional researcher? The policy analyst is usually involved in issues of concern to campus or systemwide management. The results of the policy analysis are needed immediately and may result in changes in the environment. The need of campus managers for policy analysis comes from both inside and outside the institution, from individual complaints, from government action, from demographic and social changes. The agenda of the decision maker is the source of the assignments for the policy analyst. Eventually, the policy analyst's need for data and information will influence the institutional researcher, initially in the development of short-term studies and investigations, and in the longer run in the refinement and evolution of institutional data systems that provide information suited to the analysis. The growth of interest in attrition rates is a good example. In studying program completion rates, policymakers have gone from occasionally requesting data to requiring continuous longitudinal studies.

Higher Education Planning Versus Policy Analysis

What is higher education planning? Is it a type of policy analysis or research? What is its relationship to institutional research? Donald Norris's (1991) excellent introduction to the field, *A Guide for New Planners*, describes the characteristics of various kinds of planning: strategic, long range, tactical, and operational. In a more extended discussion, Marvin Peterson (1980) defines planning as a key organizational process that may or may not be developed as part of the larger institutional management function. Peterson's definition assumes (1) that the institution and its members are concerned about the future as well as the current states of the institution and the means for achieving them, (2) that they choose to develop a planning process rather than rely on the whims of key individuals or sporadic responses to unpredictable external events, and (3) that an attempt to assess institutional strengths and weaknesses and to examine the environment for constraints and opportunities leads to changes that are beneficial to the institution's vitality.

Peterson emphasizes that planning is a process rather than a static view. Planners try to anticipate and shape the future through actions that take place in the present. They are watchful of activity in the institution's environment that may impact on the college or university, influencing its future direction. Knowledge obtained from strategic planning activities can be very beneficial to the policy analyst's need for information on environmental issues.

Planners also stimulate policy analysis. As they develop institutional goals and strategic directions, planners may discover areas of unclear or missing policy or even unearth conflicts between existing policies. In looking to the future and planning for change, planners raise issues central to the college or university—anticipated demographic changes in enrollment may require new admissions policies, for example.

Policy analysis is used in the formulation of plans, and planning suggests questions or areas in which policy analysis is needed. Planning typically leads to plans, and plans often suggest or lead to actions. Policy analysis may or may not lead to any changes, depending on the issue and the results of the analysis. Planning usually involves fairly large-scale, total system treatments; policy analysis is more focused on specific issues or questions. Planning produces plans that are finished as of particular points in time; policy analysis is repetitive and iterative as the issues and the environment change. Institutional research provides data for both planning and policy analysis, long-range forecasts, trends, and descriptions of the environment for planners, and topic- or issue-based data for policy analysts.

How does the policy analyst contribute to the work of the planner? In many cases, the policy analyst identifies issues that shape institutional goals and objectives. Because policy analysts work closely with and for decision makers, their work influences the framework that the decision maker uses to shape the planning process. Issues researched, analyzed, and studied by the policy analyst are the background of institutional planning. For example, policy analysts may identify changes in student demand as critical to the future of the institution, and the planners then incorporate into their plan a strategic emphasis on attracting a new and different market. The work of the policy analyst and the planner is interactive and interwoven, although their products may be quite distinct.

Overall, the above-named distinctions among the work of the policy analyst, the institutional researcher, and the planner may appear clear, but in day-to-day operations the distinctions blur. Many institutional researchers do all three functions, as confusing as that can sometimes be. The mindsets and assumptions required by each kind of work are different and the products differ accordingly. The harried staff member has to remember which cap is being worn and what the output should contain in order to meet the demands of the job; the ability of staff to rapidly shift administrative paradigms ensures some level of success.

Policy Analysis and the New Directions for Institutional Research Series

At present, there is no single journal for higher education policy analysis. The NDIR series is an informative source for policy analysts even though it focuses primarily on the field of institutional research. NDIR provides valuable references for data sources, techniques and tools, and descriptions of the higher education environment, including institutions and their participants. Occasionally, NDIR includes data analysis as well. We review three areas where NDIR volumes are a rich source of data, literature, and guidance to illustrate how an institutional researcher can use the series for policy analysis.

Data, Techniques, and Tools. The major strength that the institutional researcher brings to the policy analysis task is detailed student educational data: sources, methods for handling, and qualifications concerning its use. NDIR offers a number of volumes that focus on student data. For example, *Using National Data Bases* (Lenth, 1991) guides the policy analyst to major national resources. An excellent short guide to over fifty national data bases is provided in the last chapter. These national data bases are used in the first chapter to examine the policy issue of minority student participation. NDIR has not yet offered a similar volume on state-level data bases, but some of the resources cited in Lenth (1991) can be disaggregated to state-level summaries.

Besides the data sources, NDIR volumes frequently cover methodological topics, particularly new and emerging methodologies. The use of statistical and other quantitative techniques is not always simple and straightforward. The volume *Applying Statistics in Institutional Research* (Yancey, 1988) is a balanced description of the problems and opportunities inherent to the use of statistical methods. Literature for more detailed study of the methodologies is also cited, and several relatively recently applied methodologies are described. Other data-oriented volumes include *Enhancing Information Use in Decision Making* (Ewell, 1989), which alerts the policy analyst to the problem of making data meaningful to decision makers in an institution, a problem of particular concern to the policy analyst. *Alumni Research: Methods and Applications* (Melchiori, 1988) deals with a specialized subject population but provides useful information for analysts concerned with follow-up studies or more general questionnaire issues. And *Conducting Interinstitutional Comparisons* (Brinkman, 1987) provides useful cautions to the policy analyst who has data from different institutions and wishes to compare them.

Educational Context. The *Chronicle of Higher Education* is the analyst's most useful source of data on current policy problems, issues, struggles, and resolutions in higher education. Policy issues and assignments to policy analysts arise from the current events of the day. The *Chronicle* reports on those issues in a faithful and timely manner. The *Chronicle* also records the history of higher education in its making, and the longer, thoughtful analyses of current issues are the first places to look for information on educational context.

The NDIR volumes also contain descriptive information on the educational setting, particularly in relation to the central topic of each volume. Slightly dated perhaps, but still relevant for any policy analyst dealing with funding issues, is the volume *Responding to New Realities in Funding* (Leslie, 1984). Specific funding strategies and related external conditions have changed only slightly, and the organizational scheme for studying them remains relevant and current. Other, even older volumes deal with more specific events in budgeting for declining resources.

Another volume that contributes to our understanding of educational setting and context is *Assessing Academic Climates and Cultures* (Tierney, 1990). This volume contains a number of chapters that describe how to analyze an academic culture: George Kuh's chapter on student culture is particularly useful, as is Ann Austin's chapter on faculty cultures and values. Any policy analyst proposing a change in faculty governance, hiring, or compensation policy needs to have a sophisticated understanding of faculty cultures and of how to go about understanding the culture at the particular institution under study. Faculty culture at research universities is quite different from faculty culture at community colleges, but they can be analyzed and understood with some of the same tools. Estela Maria Bensimon's chapter offers the perspective of an outsider coming to a campus as the new president and illustrates a good starting point for any policy analysis.

The use of these volumes requires caution since conditions change. But the quarterly appearance of volumes in the series ensures a measure of timeliness in the topics addressed.

Other excellent discussions of academic context include those found in the Jossey-Bass series New Directions for Higher Education as well as *Academe* and more specialized journals.

Policy Analysis. NDIR volumes also include actual policy analyses. *Issues in Pricing Undergraduate Education* (Litten, 1984) studies a topic that is still of vital concern to the policy analyst. The question of how institutions should determine their undergraduate tuition levels remains a central con-cern of every independent institution and, increasingly, of every public institution. This volume summarizes several conceptual approaches to pricing issues, including the point of view of an economist who sees prices (tuition) reflecting enrollment or market demand. Pricing is also examined as a political decision—who pays and who should pay? Another volume, *The Effect of Assessment on Minority Student Participation* (Nettles, 1990), examines the twin issues of assessment and minority student participation and illustrates the interrelationships among policy issues and the impact of one policy area on another.

References

Brinkman, P. T. (ed.). *Conducting Interinstitutional Comparisons*. New Directions for Institutional Research, no. 53. San Francisco: Jossey-Bass, 1987.

Ewell, P. T. (ed.). *Enhancing Information Use in Decision Making*. New Directions for Institutional Research, no. 64. San Francisco: Jossey-Bass, 1989.

Lenth, C. S. (ed.). *Using National Data Bases*. New Directions for Institutional Research, no. 69. San Francisco: Jossey-Bass, 1991.

Leslie, L. L. (ed.). *Responding to New Realities in Funding*. New Directions for Institutional Research, no. 43. San Francisco: Jossey-Bass, 1984.

Litten, L. H. (ed.). *Issues in Pricing Undergraduate Education*. New Directions for Institutional Research, no. 42. San Francisco: Jossey-Bass, 1984.

Melchiori, G. S. (ed.). *Alumni Research: Methods and Applications*. New Directions for Institutional Research, no. 60. San Francisco: Jossey-Bass, 1988.

Muffo, J., and McLaughlin, G. *A Primer on Institutional Research*. Tallahassee, Fla.: Association for Institutional Research, 1987.

Nettles, M. T. (ed.). *The Effect of Assessment on Minority Student Participation.* New Directions for Institutional Research, no. 65. San Francisco: Jossey-Bass, 1990.

Norris, D. *A Guide for New Planners.* Ann Arbor, Mich.: Society for College and University Planners, 1991.

Peterson, M. W. "Analyzing Alternative Approaches to Planning." In P. Jedamus, M. Peterson, and Associates, *Improving Academic Management: A Handbook of Planning and Institutional Research.* San Francisco: Jossey-Bass, 1980.

Saupe, J. L. *The Functions of Institutional Research.* Tallahassee, Fla.: Association for Institutional Research, 1981.

Tierney, W. G. (ed.). *Assessing Academic Climates and Cultures.* New Directions for Institutional Research, no. 68. San Francisco: Jossey-Bass, 1990.

Yancey, B. D. (ed.). *Applying Statistics in Institutional Research.* New Directions for Institutional Research, no. 58. San Francisco: Jossey-Bass, 1988.

LAURA SAUNDERS is dean of administration at Highline Community College, Des Moines, Washington.

Policy analysis provided the framework for enrollment planning in the Arizona University System. An initial statement, developed by an analyst and approved by policymakers, serves as a guide for the new planning paradigm. Independent environmental factors are the foundation of the planning paradigm.

Enrollment Demand in Arizona: Policy Choices and Social Consequences

Stephen M. Jordan

The underlying patterns of enrollment demand throughout postsecondary education are shifting. Depending on the region of the country, these patterns are heavily influenced by a declining number of high school graduates, returning nontraditional students, ethnic minority populations becoming majorities, increasing college-going rates for women, and individual economic imperatives. Throughout the 1980s, states struggled to cope with these changes through a variety of analytical mechanisms, the most prevalent of which were demographic projections used to predict postsecondary enrollments. Unfortunately, the planning that resulted from these efforts was often based on erroneous assumptions. Consequently, many of the actions taken as a result of the planning of the 1980s were harmful. The lesson for the 1990s is that we can no longer rely on simple demographic models that translate the college-age population figure into college enrollment projections (Frances, 1989).

A New Planning Paradigm

The Arizona University System was facing the prospect of significantly increasing enrollments. How many students? Unknown. From which socioeconomic backgrounds? Unknown. In what geographical regions of the state? Unknown. We had a sense of an impending enrollment explosion, but we did not know when or why. And, most important, we were unsure of the consequences of the policy interventions that we might choose to employ to meet future enrollment growth. We were concerned that unintended consequences would have as important an effect as the intended purposes of our policy preferences.

Clearly, a new planning paradigm was needed for examining enrollment growth in a systematic and comprehensive way, a paradigm capable of considering the interactive effects of changes in the demographic characteristics of the population, as well as its size; changes in education and student aid policies; changes in economic, social, and political trends; and changes in individual institutional management strategies. In October 1989, the chair of the Strategic Planning Committee of the Board of Regents and I authored a memorandum to the board in which we enumerated four principles for planning for enrollment growth: (1) Provide access to higher education for all residents of Arizona who meet reasonable admissions standards. (2) Admission of qualified nonresident students benefits Arizona residents by creating academic, social, and cultural diversity and provides important economic support to the university system and Arizona's general economy. (3) Provide high-quality educational opportunities to students, engage in productive research in support of humanity in general and the citizens of the state of Arizona in particular, and provide public service in support of the aims and objectives of Arizona's citizens. (4) Expand higher education in Arizona through cooperation between the university system and the community college system.

The memorandum also included assumptions about growth and an extensive list of short- and long-term strategies that might be implemented to manage enrollment growth. Following the release of the document, the Strategic Planning Committee chair and I met individually with each member of the board and with each university president to review the principles, assumptions, strategies, and constraints enumerated in the memorandum. The memorandum became, in effect, the foundation on which we decided to build our new planning paradigm.

The paradigm was framed within the context of the system's strategic plan for enrollment growth. Stated simply, the plan is to enable the Arizona public universities to meet the baccalaureate and graduate student educational needs of Arizona through the next twenty years. It consists of four objectives: (1) to estimate the enrollment demand to the year 2010, (2) to estimate the optimum enrollment capacity at our existing university campuses and strategies for meeting this capacity, (3) to develop system strategies for meeting potential enrollment demands, and (4) to evaluate the resource needs and potential sources of funds of the various strategies.

The board of regents formally adopted the five-year strategic plan for the Arizona University System in September 1990. The board restated its commitment to providing access to higher education to all residents of Arizona who meet the admissions standards. Additionally, the continued admission of qualified, nonresident students to the three universities was encouraged since these students benefit Arizona residents by creating academic, social, and cultural diversity and provide important economic support to the university system and to the general economy of the state. The board also established the principle of expansion of higher education in Arizona through cooperation between the public university system and the public community college system. Finally, in addition to this strategic direction—planning for enrollment growth—the plan includes five other system strategic directions: undergraduate education, graduate education and research, economic development and public service, diversity, and acquisition and utilization of resources.

Enrollment Demand Model. The unique aspect of the planning paradigm is the development of a new enrollment demand model. The model has been built using the system dynamics approach with the intent of producing a powerful new way to look at higher education policy options. System dynamics is a computer simulation modeling approach that permits examination of the interactions among complex social systems. Central to the approach is the concept of feedback.

In the past, decision makers have been plagued by the unintended consequences of their actions. The system dynamics model enables decision makers to take a broader view of their policy options and to develop a keener understanding of the probable outcomes of their choices—in this case, the effect on enrollment demand. For example, most state enrollment projection models are driven primarily by in-state demographic trends, yet close to four-fifths of the population growth of Arizona comes from net immigration. Consequently, the model must be able to encompass more complex interrelationships between demographic and economic trends at the state, regional, and national levels.

At the outset, we made a specific distinction between *potential demand* and *expected demand*. Conceptually, potential demand exists among qualified people able to benefit from a college education if barriers to their enrollment are removed (such as lack of academic preparation or inability to pay for college). Expected demand is the most likely projection of enrollment demand considering both the removal of existing barriers and the potential creation of new barriers. It is the demand that we project will be placed on higher education in Arizona during the planning period. We intend to use the model to examine the Arizona enrollment demand implications of changes in policy at the national, state, and institutional levels and the resulting shifts in students from potential demand to actual enrollment.

In building the model, the first step was to take a broad view of a continuum of factors affecting or driving the demand for higher education (see Figure 4.1). The seven groups of factors identified fell into three categories. The first category includes factors over which Arizonans have very little control, such as demographic, economic, and political trends. The second category includes intermediate factors that Arizona institutions do not control but may influence. These include student perceptions of accessibility to college, which in turn may affect student motivation and prepa-

Figure 4.1. Continuum of Factors
Affecting the Demand for Higher Education

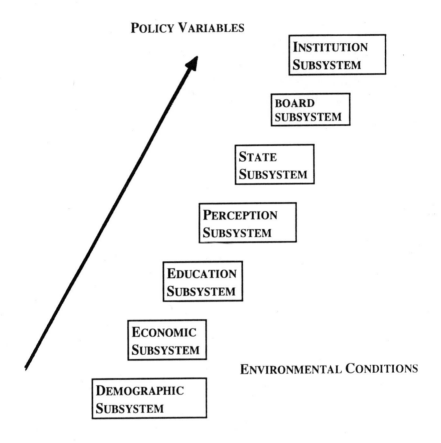

POLICY VARIABLES

INSTITUTION
SUBSYSTEM

BOARD
SUBSYSTEM

STATE
SUBSYSTEM

PERCEPTION
SUBSYSTEM

EDUCATION
SUBSYSTEM

ECONOMIC
SUBSYSTEM

ENVIRONMENTAL CONDITIONS

DEMOGRAPHIC
SUBSYSTEM

ration for college-level work. The third category includes factors over which
Arizonans generally have more control, including state-level education
funding policies; board-level policies such as tuition, residence requirements, and minority recruitment; and, finally, institution-level policies,
such as admissions standards, student aid policies, and graduation criteria.
Each of the seven major groups of factors influencing demand for college
was incorporated into a separate subsystem in the model.

The second step in building the model was to talk with participants
from the Arizona universities in order to identify measurable variables of
the factors driving demand for college education, and then to specify the
relationships among them. Here we looked at the effect that one variable
driving demand has on another variable that also drives demand. In a
positive relationship, both variables move in the same direction. For example, an increase in student grants increases the demand for college. In a

negative relationship, the variables move in opposite directions. For example, increases in the wages earned in jobs that do not require a college education decrease the demand for college. In developing the model, particular attention was paid to the effects of economic recessions on higher education enrollments. The model was programmed to consider the historical impact of recessions that have increased enrollments, under the assumption that there would be two recessions during the twenty-year planning period.

The third step was a substantial data collection effort. Much of the data used in building the model come from standard compilations that the Arizona universities generate on a routine basis. The universities also ran special computer programs to generate data used to calculate college-going rates detailed by age and ethnicity, a central component of the model. Environmental trend data, including the 1990 census, were collected from state and national agencies. These data were analyzed extensively to provide additional insights into the factors that are likely to affect future demand for higher education in Arizona.

Analytically, it was necessary to begin by measuring current enrollment by race, ethnicity, and age and to anchor the figures in a baseline year. We chose 1990 as the base year because we could anchor all our demographic data to the new national census data. Application of the college-going rates of Arizona resident students by race and ethnicity to the age and race population groups developed from the 1990 census data provides one measure of projected enrollment for college education in Arizona, assuming no change in participation rates by race, ethnicity, age, or residence status. The next step was to determine the most likely enrollment by estimating changes in college-going rates based on our current Arizona college-going rates and relating them to the rate of change in the national college-going rates by race and ethnicity over a fourteen-year period.

As a result of our efforts, we are projecting four-year-university sector enrollments to increase by 55,000 students by the year 2010, an increase of 57 percent. The enrollment increases will be distributed as 79 percent coming from residents and 21 percent from nonresidents. Total postsecondary enrollments are projected to increase 146,000 by 2010, a 58 percent increase.

There appear to be three principal reasons for these high projections. First, the population projections by the universities' planners and the official Arizona State population projections are consistent in projecting average state population growth of 2 to 3 percent per year for the twenty-year period. The continuation of existing participation rates with the projected increases in population results in large increases in expected demand. Second, Arizona has a relatively young population, which will affect the traditional college-age eighteen- to twenty-four-year-old cohort during the planning period and further increase enrollments. Third, Arizona will see significant increases in enrollments as a result of large, traditionally underrepresented minorities moving toward majorities.

Optimum Enrollment Capacity. Each public university completed a capacity study to determine the optimum headcount enrollment capacity of its main campus, the second component of the paradigm. The studies examined the histories and cultures of the institutions, their mission statements and visions, key enrollment trends in the past decade, faculty and student opinions, proposed future enrollment profiles, and inventories of current and required space needs based on the institutions' five-year capital improvement plans and the guidelines of the Council for Educational Facility Planners International. On the basis of these studies, the three university presidents recommended that enrollments on the main campus sites be downsized at Arizona State University from 41,000 students to 39,000 students, that enrollments remain at the current 35,000 students at the University of Arizona, and that Northern Arizona University grow by another 1,500 students from 14,500 to 16,000. The enrollment capacity studies were viewed as a cornerstone of the paradigm because the mathematics of enrollment growth is simple: Enrollment demand minus capacity equals unmet need.

Strategies to Meet Enrollment Demand. The projections for enrollment growth, which is the third component of the paradigm, set the stage for the range of alternatives presently being considered. The alternatives were developed by a working group consisting of representatives from the three universities and the Board of Regents Central Office. Members of the working group included a vice president for student affairs, chief university planning officers, institutional research officers, and faculty from higher education programs within the colleges of education. The working group prepared the alternatives for review by the presidents of the three universities and the executive director of the board of regents sitting as the Council of Presidents. The alternatives were then presented to the board of regents.

These alternatives can be categorized into three groups: internal, non-capital-intensive; external, non-capital-intensive; and external, capital-intensive. In categorizing the alternatives in this way, we are attempting to look at a continuum of ways in which we might accommodate additional growth, beginning with our existing campuses' physical plants, moving to academic and physical alternatives exclusive of our campuses, and ending with construction of new campuses.

Internal, Non-Capital-Intensive. In the category of internal, non-capital-intensive strategies, we are examining alternatives such as evening and weekend colleges, a trimester system, increased financial assistance to accelerate student progress toward degrees, increased faculty workload effort, differentiated admissions standards, and increased classroom utilization.

Two general themes are inherent to these alternatives. The first is, Should we and can we make better utilization of our existing physical plants? The second is, Should we and can we modify the demand for utilizing our existing campuses? There are clearly implications for the roles and missions of our existing campuses, given our traditional views of access and our perceptions of quality. To the extent that we move toward better utilization of our existing campuses, we run into conflict with our capacity studies that recommend capping or downsizing our three existing campuses in order to preserve quality. To the extent that we differentiate admissions, we conflict with our traditional values in Arizona that hold that an academically qualified resident student should be permitted to attend any of the three universities that she or he chooses.

External, Non-Capital-Intensive. In the category of external, non-capital-intensive strategies, we are examining alternatives such as enhanced educational opportunities for Arizona residents to attend institutions in other states through expanded participation in the exchange programs sponsored by the Western Interstate Commission for Higher Education (WICHE). In the WICHE student exchange programs, western states agree to accept students in designated graduate and undergraduate programs in exchange for the right to send students to programs designated by other states. We also are examining enhanced opportunities for Arizona residents through direct contracts with governing boards of other four-year institutions in other states that have excess capacity. Encouragement of support for independent education by providing state-supported student aid to Arizona residents attending independent institutions in Arizona is a third alternative being examined. Also under consideration is shared university facilities funded by local communities. In addition, expanded corporate education similar to Motorola University, a corporate-sponsored program with curriculum and faculty provided by the local community colleges, is being considered. And, finally, we are looking at possibilities for expanding opportunities at community colleges, similar to our Northern Arizona University-Yuma/Arizona Western College (community college) model. This alternative calls for the development of a consortia campus system that would be composed of a series of university centers or branch campuses located on or adjacent to the campuses of community colleges across Arizona. While retaining their individual institutional identities, management systems, and governance structures, the universities and the community colleges would form a system of educational consortia by means of intergovernmental agreements, mission statements, articulation agreements, transfer contracts, and telecommunications linkages through which baccalaureate degree programs on a 2 + 2 basis might be offered.

Obviously, the external, non-capital-intensive alternatives all focus on avoiding or shifting the cost of additional capital facilities by contracting with other states, by encouraging local communities to determine their needs and invite universities to offer programs in community-provided facilities, by cooperating with businesses, and by sharing existing facilities with community colleges. These alternatives seem to fall between our traditional notions of continuing education and branch campuses.

External, Capital-Intensive. The third category of strategies being considered is composed of external, capital-intensive alternatives. In this category, we are considering four alternatives: (1) a new liberal arts campus of five thousand students, (2) a branch campus or campuses of five thousand to ten thousand students, (3) a comprehensive baccalaureate and master's degree granting state college of five thousand to ten thousand students, and (4) a comprehensive, limited doctorate-granting university of ten thousand students. The liberal arts campus consideration derives from public concerns regarding the condition of undergraduate education as expressed in a number of major national reports issued during the 1980s and in the board of regents' own strategic direction on undergraduate education. The branch campus concept is a continuation of a direction already initiated in Arizona with the development of the Arizona State University-West Campus as an upper-division and graduate campus of Arizona State University. A comprehensive state college would offer an alternative currently not available in Arizona. It would focus on excellence in teaching, strong student services, and public service, and it would encourage student participation in all areas of campus life. In all three alternatives, we are considering governance structures in which the chief executive officer of the new campus would report to the president of an existing university. In the liberal arts and the state college alternatives, we also are considering free-standing campuses, with the chief executive officer reporting directly to the board of regents, as well as the possibility of separate governing boards for new campuses.

The comprehensive, limited doctorate-granting university would continue the public sector tradition of offering only university-level postsecondary education in Arizona, with a primary emphasis on undergraduate education, smaller class sizes, and limited research. The doctoral programs would evolve over time, growing from the strength of academic programs at the undergraduate and master's levels. The only governance structure contemplated under this alternative is for the chief executive officer to report directly to the board of regents.

Clearly, expansion of campuses has implications for the roles and missions of our existing campuses as we contemplate expanding the size of the public four-year sector. In Arizona, we have taken pride in the simplicity of our governance system—three separate and distinct universities reporting to one governing board. Implementation of these strategies would begin a process of developing university systems within a system or of creating multiple governing boards for the public four-year sector. If the new institutions are created within the governance structure of the existing universities, governance of those universities would become more complex. If the new institutions are created under separate boards, the opportunity for competitiveness among institutions reporting to separate boards is enhanced. In either case, our existing universities will be affected.

Policy Choices and Social Consequences. We have examined the social consequences of a number of our policy choices, including the effects of closing the participation rate gap between majority and ethnic minority students, increasing the transfer rate from community colleges to the universities, increasing the graduation rates of high school students, and limiting enrollments. Through the use of our model, we have been able to examine the consequences of modifying existing policies or barriers to enrollments and their implications to our expected enrollment demand increase of 55,000 students by the year 2010. We are using "what if" analysis to examine both the impacts of outcomes that we would like to achieve and the harmful influences that we would like to mitigate. The ultimate outcome that we seek is development of a plan to implement one or more of our strategies.

Closing the Participation Rate Gap. Perhaps one of the most important findings to come from the new paradigm has been the implications of the potential effects of the shifts in race, ethnicity, and age in the population projections on enrollment demand. We examined the implications of policies designed not only to encourage minority participation in postsecondary education but also to close the gap between majority and minority participation rates. Currently, there are 40,000 minority students participating in postsecondary education in Arizona. By the year 2010, the projected demand will increase the number of minority students by 75,000 to a total of 115,000 due to population growth and the change in ethnic distribution of the population. Closure of the current gap in participation rates by 50 percent will increase demand by an additional 23,000 students by the year 2010; elimination of the gap will increase demand by 46,000 students over the expected minority student base of 115,000. Hence, the elimination of barriers to participation in higher education may increase minority enrollment demand by 20 to 40 percent. In summary, we have found that for Arizona, future enrollment demand depends more on race, ethnicity, age distribution, and rates of participation than simply on the highs and lows of our total state population projections.

Increasing Community College Transfer Rates. There is a significant relationship between the community college and university sectors in Arizona. Many of the community colleges have registration processes that permit a student to jointly register at a community college and a university. The relationship has been further enhanced by the development of an articulation agreement between the community colleges and the universities that is based on a course equivalence guide. A student can register for a course at a community college and know at the time of registration whether it is transferable to the universities.

Because it is easy for students to cross-register, and even to transfer from the community college to a university, back again to a community college, and then back again to a university, estimates of the number of students who transfer from community colleges to the universities are not precise. This phenomenon of cross-registration and transferring has become known as "swirling." It has resulted in the universities having to rely heavily on the community college system to provide the lower-division coursework for many of our students. Swirling makes the task of estimating the number of annual transfers from the community college sector difficult. However, our estimates are that five thousand students per year transfer from the community college sector to the three universities. If the numbers were doubled, and if these students persisted at the universities, the additional demand would result in an almost 16 percent increase to our baseline projection of fifty-five thousand additional students between the years 1990 and 2010.

Increasing High School Graduation Rates. Arizona currently graduates 64 percent of its high school students. If present efforts such as the Governor's Task Force on Education Reform are successful and result in an increase of the graduation rate to at least the national average of 74 percent, higher education enrollments will increase by three thousand students per year. However, when the pooling effect of these students is considered over the lifetime of their postsecondary experiences, enrollment demand is estimated to increase in excess of ten thousand students.

Enrollment Caps. The numerous effects of enrollment caps are both positive and negative. Caps would most likely result in a change of the apportionment of the resident-nonresident mix, necessarily increasing admissions standards and improving educational program quality and prestige. Implicit in the improved education program quality and prestige is an assumption that we would experience improved graduation rates. Enrollment caps also may result in reduced dropout rates.

On the negative side, enrollment caps may result in fewer minority students in the universities, unless the caps are accompanied by significant efforts to strengthen preparation for university-level work and enhanced recruitment and retention programs. Caps also might have a negative effect on the Arizona economy. With fewer residents prepared for higher-value jobs, the state will experience slower economic growth. The consequences for the state would be a smaller tax base, less capacity to deliver services, and smaller gains in quality of life compared to the rest of the nation.

Conclusion

Traditional methods of estimating future enrollments have not been successful. Frances (1989) has documented and explained many of the reasons for the failure of past demographic modeling efforts and has suggested the need to consider other trends, including changes in education and student aid policies, changes in economic, social, and political trends, and changes in individual institutional management strategies (Frances, 1990).

Ultimately, our success at planning for enrollment growth will be judged by the convergence of the services that we end up providing with the demand for those services. It is one thing to anticipate demand, another to plan for demand, and a third to meet demand. A new planning paradigm that considers these elements within the broadest framework of strategic planning will bring about the kind of policy analysis and implementation that will permit higher education to be more cognizant of the social consequences of its policy initiatives. Arizona has begun implementing such a paradigm. Our success or failure will not only define the prospects for the vitality and relevance of Arizona's public university system for the next half century but may well also define the social and economic fabric of the state.

References

Frances, C. "Uses and Misuses of Demographic Projections: Lessons for the 1990s." In A. Levine and Associates, *Shaping Higher Education's Future: Demographic Realities and Opportunities, 1990–2000.* San Francisco: Jossey-Bass, 1989.

Frances, C. "Key Economic Indicators for Higher Education." In K. H. Hanson and J. W. Meyerson (eds.), *Higher Education in a Changing Economy.* New York: Macmillan, 1990.

STEPHEN M. JORDAN is deputy executive director for finance and planning for the Arizona Board of Regents and adjunct professor in the College of Education, Division of Educational Leadership and Policy Studies, Arizona State University, Tempe.

Sexual harassment raises new and challenging policy issues.

Reassessing Effective Procedures in Cases of Sexual Harassment

Steven G. Olswang

That sexual harassment of students by faculty exists on college and university campuses is no longer a debatable question. Studies indicate varying levels of sexual harassment on campus, but all conclude that the problem is prevalent (Dzeich and Weiner, 1984; Kenig and Ryan, 1986; Fitzgerald and others, 1988). And while the problem has existed on campuses for a long time, few reports of sexual harassment are made when compared to the incidence level (Robertson, Dyer, and Campbell, 1988; Schneider, 1987).

Few institutions have experience in investigating allegations of sexual harassment or taking action against faculty where violations have been identified. Institutional responses have been to use campus procedures that exist for investigating allegations of other forms of discrimination (such as race or disability based), or for disciplining faculty for violations of the terms of their contracts. This latter response usually follows the guidelines for faculty due process enunciated in the policies of the American Association of University Professors (AAUP, 1983). Recently, separate policies have evolved, including specific guidelines from the American Council on Education (1986) and the AAUP (1990), for dealing with sexual harassment cases.

When the issue of sexual harassment arises, the traditional forms of addressing complaints and assigning punishment may not be practical or appropriate. Indeed, some authors believe that traditional university procedures are to blame for the low numbers of women students who file reports against faculty (Riger, 1991).

The responsibility for the adoption of formal policies or procedures generally rests with an institutional governing body, such as its board of trustees, or by delegated authority with the president of the university.

However, the historical model of collegial governance, still prevalent at most institutions, requires the involvement of faculty in the development of policies and procedures, particularly those that could potentially affect the terms and conditions of faculty employment. Policies on sexual harassment, definitions of causes for discipline, and due process procedures for reviewing faculty misconduct are clearly matters in which faculty expect to participate.

Historically, policies have been developed in isolation from elements external to the faculty environment. However, exclusion of external factors is no longer possible. For example, state laws may mandate certain practices. These laws may include administrative procedures acts, which delineate due process procedures applicable to internal investigative and adjudicative proceedings; public disclosure laws, which open up personnel and hearing files to the public; and state discrimination laws, which delegate to other agencies the responsibility to address such claims.

Of equal concern is the growing perception by the public that faculty have not been held accountable for their actions. State legislators and independent institutional boards have exerted greater oversight of faculty activities in recent years, and students will no longer tolerate being blocked out of processes that affect them. Overall, the ability of faculty to operate in isolation from these external forces has been substantially restricted. Nowhere is this more evident than in situations involving the sexual harassment of students by faculty.

Case Example: University of Washington

In 1989 at the University of Washington, a woman student, following the long-established university procedure for reporting a violation of its sexual harassment policy, filed a formal complaint with the university's Human Rights Office. Headed by the assistant provost and equal employment officer, this office is designated to receive and investigate formal complaints of sexual harassment by faculty (as well as other allegations of discrimination, including those based on race, gender, national origin, and so on). Note that pursuant to Title IX of the Education Amendments of 1972 (20 U.S.C. 1680 et seq.) and Title VII of the Civil Rights Act of 1964 (42 U.S.C. 2000 et seq.), institutions that receive federal funds are precluded from discriminating against any individual on the basis of sex and are required to have institutional grievance procedures in place to address such violations. Sexual harassment is, of course, just one form of sex discrimination (*Alexander* v. *Yale University* [459 F. Supp. 1 (D. Conn. 1977), affirmed 631 F.2d 178 (2nd Cir. 1980)] and *Meritor Savings Bank* v. *Vinson* [477 U.S. 57 (1986)]).

The student initially filed her complaint after being subjected to what she claimed was a series of unwanted and unwelcome sexual requests and improper touches by a senior faculty member. The faculty member vigorously denied engaging in any such actions. While the university's Human Rights Office was conducting its normal investigation, the faculty member and his family took out public advertisements in the student newspaper, naming the student and listing, in detail, the student's allegations, including those about the professor's sexually explicit requests and conduct. The professor's family also distributed leaflets on campus, describing the student's complaints and demanding that she take a lie detector test. These actions created substantial distress for the student victim and precluded the university's ability to maintain the confidentiality of the process. They also prompted the student to file a lawsuit against the institution. The publicity in the student newspaper (and, subsequently, in the local media) deprived her, she claimed, of her right to continue her education. She was no longer able to continue her bachelors' degree program because the atmosphere had been poisoned by the faculty member's deliberate actions.

The university, nonetheless, continued its internal investigation of the student's complaint. Because the student was by then suing the university, she and her attorney were unwilling to cooperate without a settlement up front. Because the faculty member was named by the university as a defendant in the lawsuit (in an attempt to shift the liability, for if acts of sexual harassment and retaliation were committed, he was responsible and not the university), he also was unfriendly to the university. Despite these difficulties, the university completed its investigation with the Human Rights Office concluding that sexual harassment had occurred. The dean of the college independently evaluated the findings and concurred that sexual harassment had occurred. The dean then initiated termination proceedings against the faculty member.

A committee composed solely of faculty members was appointed by the faculty senate to adjudicate the dismissal charge. The burden of proving that sexual harassment had occurred rested with the university. The faculty member employed an attorney who compelled the adjudication committee to follow practices familiar to civil lawsuits, but unfamiliar to processes designated as collegial. As a result of this intensive legal maneuvering, over a year passed before the first faculty hearing took place. During all of this time, the faculty member, who had been removed from teaching to protect students, remained on the university payroll.

The hearing took twenty-two days, spread out over two months. Some months later, the faculty committee issued a finding of "no cause" to believe sexual harassment had occurred. In essence, the faculty committee found that the professor was more credible than the student. Because most of the alleged sexual incidents were not witnessed (although some were), the committee concluded that the student should not be believed over a tenured faculty member. This faculty committee finding was appealed by the college dean to the president. Almost a year and a half after the student first filed her complaint, the president upheld the faculty committee decision that no harassment had occurred and ordered the reinstatement of the faculty member.

As noted earlier, the advertisements in the student newspaper taken out by the faculty member and his family made the formal complaint a very public matter. The Human Rights Office's investigation report, the hearing committee's finding, and the president's decision were declared public documents under state public records laws and released to the press. Ironically, as a result of this publicity, a former graduate student, who some ten years prior had had a year-long sexual involvement with the accused faculty member, came forward to provide additional confirmation of this faculty member's propensity to engage students in sexual activity. Although this former student came forward after the final decision, the president, in the light of the new evidence, remanded the matter back to the faculty adjudication committee for a new hearing.

Again several months passed, followed by a number of days of hearings with all sides represented by legal counsel. The faculty adjudication committee found that this new testimony totally contradicted the faculty member's assertions that he was true to his wife and that he never had been sexually involved with a student. Nonetheless, the all-faculty committee, despite the finding that it was "a closer call" and that the faculty member's reputation was "sullied," concluded that the faculty member was still more credible than the student and that there was still no cause to believe that sexual harassment had occurred.

This decision was again appealed by the dean to the president. This time, the president remanded the matter back to the faculty committee, concluding that the evidence in the record was perhaps not quite in line with the interpretation placed on it by the committee. The president posed very specific questions to the committee about the evidence and asked them to respond in thirty days. The faculty committee told the president that they would take as long as they wanted, for justice takes time. Now, three years after the initial complaint was filed, the matter rested a third time with the faculty adjudication committee.

In the interim, the university settled the litigation with the student by facilitating her completion of a degree at another institution and by paying substantial damages, costs, and attorney's fees. The university's liability stemmed not from the faculty member's sexual harassment but from its publication of the paid advertisements in the student newspaper and its inability to internally resolve the matter on a timely basis.

The faculty adjudication committee solicited additional information from the parties involved. After five months from the date the president remanded the matter back for clarification, the adjudication committee responded that it weighed the evidence in a manner consistent with its earlier conclusion. Finding that the university administration did not meet its burden of proof, the faculty adjudication committee determined that the faculty member should not be dismissed. The president, immediately upon receipt of the opinion, issued his decision reinstating the faculty member to all rights and privileges.

The obvious fallout from this process on both institutional reputation and institutional operation is significant. The disruption in the academic unit from which this faculty member and student came, with its faculty and students taking sides and acting as witnesses, has been devastating. The student was driven out of the institution, and despite the institution's attempt to strictly follow its own procedures in addressing the allegation, it could not control the public disclosure by the faculty member or the media. Even though the student was able to complete her degree elsewhere and received a significant amount in monetary damages for her suffering, the matter is not fully resolved. The student government, angry over the faculty member's reinstatement, has announced it will picket his classes in the future.

Concerns over Traditional University Process

The Fourteenth Amendment of the U.S. Constitution provides that faculty members in public institutions have property interests in their tenured positions that cannot be removed without prior due process of law (*Board of Regents* v. *Roth* [408 U.S. 564 (1972)] and *Perry* v. *Sindermann* [408 U.S. 593 (1972)]. In independent institutions, tenure is a contract right that cannot be terminated without contractual liability. The intent of standard academic faculty disciplinary procedures is to internalize a fair due process structure without incorporating the enormously complex elements found in civil litigation.

This case example demonstrates the obsolescence of the idea that loosely structured, faculty-only collegial reviews work in situations where a faculty member's job is at stake. The intrusion of legal processes requires that universities make their processes more professional. While faculty may be capable of assessing the facts, they are not capable of managing a complex legal proceeding. Further, a process reliant on voluntary faculty service is ill-equipped to address any matter in a timely fashion.

In addition, the perception that faculty protect their own is a concern that will not be overcome with a process in which faculty remain the sole judges of their peers' conduct. Victims, whether students or staff, are demanding participation, or at least fairness and neutrality. Institutional liability for a failure to resolve issues in a timely fashion dictates administrative management of an otherwise collegial process.

In recognition of the adverse publicity generated by the University of Washington case, and the shared frustration by the faculty adjudication committee and faculty leadership, a process was initiated to review the procedures. The faculty senate chair and the university president appointed an administrator-faculty committee to review the broad system of due process on campus. The committee was appointed in summer 1991, even as the adjudication of the case continued.

The committee membership included faculty expertise in the area of legal and administrative procedures and policy, administrative expertise in personnel matters, and representation and advice from the state attorney general responsible for protecting the legal interests of the university and its faculty. The committee's mandate was to examine institutional faculty due process procedures. The struggle within the committee was to consider the traditional involvement of faculty in the process, and to ensure that state administrative procedures act requirements are met and that all procedures permit *timely* consideration of the concerns of all parties involved, not just those of the faculty member accused of the violation. Thus, at issue was how to continue the traditional role of faculty and yet eliminate the appearance of faculty bias, while providing for the presence of sufficient expertise in administering the requirements of the law.

The committee worked diligently for five months trying to develop an integrated practice that it could recommend for further review to the faculty and administration. The committee's conclusions identified a new model of due process procedures, meeting all of the diverse requirements.

This model has several components. In meeting the requirement that faculty be consulted in matters involving the continuation of appointment of a colleague when he or she is faced with allegations of violation of ethical standards or terms of employment, the design proposes that before a formal charge is made by an administrator, the faculty will be consulted. They are to serve as an internal review body, advising the provost on whether or not, based on the evidence collected, justification exists to take formal disciplinary or dismissal action.

A striking recommendation is that a neutral third party be used to carry out the process. This individual would be mutually selected by the administration and faculty and act as an institutional hearing officer. Because of the legal requirements for due process, this individual would have to have legal training. Thus, the individual would be qualified to conduct a due process hearing, thereby eliminating the need for the faculty to oversee the procedure. The faculty members would serve more as a panel of jurors, with the hearing officer sitting as the judge, making legal rulings, and running the proceedings. The burden of proof would still remain on the administration, as it should. The findings of the hearing would go to the provost for a decision, which could be appealed to the president.

Even more striking is the recommendation that the panel need not be composed only of faculty members. For example, if the allegation concerns sexual harassment against a student, the panel would be faculty and students; if against a staff member, the panel would be staff and faculty. Thus, the concept that the fact finders should be peers is expanded to include the peers of victims, not just the peers of the accused.

Together, these recommendations represent a radical change from standard institutional practices as well as from the policies of the AAUP. The model recognizes that the faculty are not equipped to run autonomous faculty disciplinary procedures in the current legal and political environment of universities and colleges. Instead, the model places the adjudication process in the hands of an individual trained to fairly administer the rigid requirements of a due process hearing, one who is not appointed by the faculty alone. Furthermore, with a singular hearing officer controlling the process, the delay inevitably resulting from a faculty committee is removed, thereby fostering timely resolution of disputes. The model also recognizes that faculty must share the responsibility of assessing faculty conduct with members of other constituencies.

This model is now being reviewed by faculty, the administration, and the student government. Some faculty still strongly hold the view that faculty only ought to sit with the hearing officer, yet students and staff equally desire representation when they are victims. Only time will tell as to the final outcome.

Conclusion

Bad cases may make bad law, yet, in this situation, a bad case has prompted an institution to reflect on itself. When things do not go right, the choices are to ignore the problem, study it, or change it. In this instance, the institution chose to critically assess its failure. Employing its existing governance structures, the institution was able to identify the deficiencies in its own process and recommend a new model that balances the evolving legal requirements with the traditional expectation of faculty participation.

This story is not yet complete, but it is a good indicator of the type of institutional reassessment that must go on when circumstances change. The historical precedent of protecting academic freedom and tenure from external subject matter or political intrusion is not the common form of due process problems that arises in modern universities. Thus, the principle of exclusive faculty control over matters of academic freedom and tenure can no longer be sacrosanct. The realization that the perception and reality are different is crucial to effecting change. Indeed, it took a difficult case, with enormous amounts of bad publicity and substantial legal liability, to shock all parties out of complacency that everything was working when in fact it was not. The use of neutral third parties, patterned after the process of civil law, may bring a lessening of control by faculty. However, it is a valid response to the realization that in certain circumstances, particularly those involving sexual harassment, faculty are not qualified to act as judge and jury.

Whether these collegial changes in process will ultimately be adopted is yet to be determined. But like any ongoing evaluation based on data sources at hand, learning and change inevitably result.

References

American Association of University Professors. "Recommended Institutional Regulations on Academic Freedom and Tenure." *Academe,* 1983, *69,* 15A–20A.

American Association of University Professors. "Sexual Harassment: Suggested Policy and Procedures for Handling Complaints." *Academe,* 1990, *76,* 42–43.

American Council on Education. *Sexual Harassment on Campus: Suggestions for Reviewing Campus Policy and Educational Programs.* Washington, D.C.: American Council on Education, 1986.

Dzeich, B. W., and Weiner, L. *The Lecherous Professor.* Boston: Beacon Press, 1984.

Fitzgerald, L. F., and others. "The Incidence and Dimensions of Sexual Harassment in Academia and the Workplace." *Journal of Vocational Behavior,* 1988, *32,* 152–175.

Kenig, S., and Ryan, J. "Sex Differences in Levels of Tolerance and Attribution of Blame for Sexual Harassment on a University Campus." *Sex Roles,* 1986, *15,* 535–549.

Riger, S. "Gender Dilemmas in Sexual Harassment Policies and Procedures." *American Psychologist,* 1991, *46,* 497–505.

Robertson, C., Dyer, C. E., and Campbell, D. "Campus Harassment: Sexual Harassment Policies and Procedures at Institutions of Higher Learning." *Signs,* 1988, *13,* 792–812.

Schneider, B. E. "Graduate Women, Sexual Harassment, and University Policy." *Journal of Higher Education,* 1987, *58,* 46–65.

STEVEN G. OLSWANG *is vice provost and professor of educational leadership and policy studies in the College of Education at the University of Washington, Seattle.*

The University of California at Berkeley will need to appoint 1,543 new faculty between 1987 and 2006. A potential shortage of faculty and scarce resources led to policy analysis of the management of faculty positions. The Berkeley culture of decentralized decision making and significant faculty involvement led to the development of a new model of management.

Facing Realities: Planning for Faculty Needs in a Major Research University

Roslyn R. Elms

The task of managing faculty positions at a university is relatively easy when an institution has a moderate growth rate and when there is a plentiful supply of faculty candidates to recruit. This has been the experience in higher education institutions for the last fifteen years. Major research universities lured the "stars," created centers of excellence across their campuses, and relished the ability to have both breadth and depth. Looking back, we see that it was a very good time.

What of the future? Predictions of faculty shortages are national news. There is widespread concern about the large numbers of faculty reaching retirement age when interest in academic careers is waning and replacement candidates are scarce. There is continuous growth in the eligible student population in many states, especially in public institutions. Current federal and state budget deficits are creating crisis management conditions, and academic planning efforts are falling victim to situational expediencies. Looking forward, we can see that difficult times lie ahead for higher education.

Most of the discussions about future needs for faculty have focused on national trends, and the analyses have involved aggregated statistical information. The dialogue has been informative and it has succeeded in focusing public attention on the issue. But faculty are hired at institutions. It is on the campus that the jobs exist, and even within the same system or the same state, campus needs for faculty vary widely. Some campuses do not anticipate problems replacing faculty. On the other hand, issues of faculty replacement are not unique to any university (Bowen and Schuster, 1986; Bowen and Sosa, 1989; Chatman and Jung, 1991; and Gamson, Finnegan, and Youn, 1990).

Objective of Analysis

The institutional perspective is central to planning effectively for faculty replacement. Most colleges and universities are already planning for the next century, and the need for new faculty to replace retirees or to meet enrollment increases is the central issue in that planning. In 1990, it became clear that a reexamination of the faculty replacement process on the University of California at Berkeley campus was needed. This chapter describes the efforts of the Berkeley campus to understand and plan for faculty replacement.

The policy analysis work on faculty replacement at the University of California at Berkeley identified several interdependent themes: (1) Retirements are not an isolated variable but rather one important factor in a complex social matrix. (2) Student enrollments affect faculty replacement needs. (3) The need for gender and ethnic diversity within the faculty will continue to exert pressure on faculty replacement efforts. And (4) campus differences, within the university system, demand creative responses to the challenge of faculty replacement.

To understand how Berkeley is proceeding to revise its management of faculty positions, it is important to understand the campus. It is part of a multicampus system in a state that has supported and been generous to public higher education for over one hundred years.

Background: Environment and Problem Statement

The University of California system, headed by a president, is a constitutional university of eight general campuses and one health sciences campus. By public mandate, it is the research university for the state and it has been granted exclusive authority to award doctoral degrees within the public sector. The system has standardized salary scales, retirement and employee benefits, and other uniform personnel policies.

The 1992 fiscal year state budget for the University of California was $2.3 billion. Faculty positions are generated by enrollment, using a formula that was negotiated in the 1970s between the university and the state. Except for health sciences programs that have categorical funding, the formula does not recognize discipline, level, or method of teaching. The state funds lower- and upper-division undergraduates, all levels of graduate students, and laboratories and lectures without consideration of related differences in the teaching costs. Differential program funding is made by the system office in the allocation funding process. For example, in allocating instructional funds, the Office of the President considers the proportion of graduate to undergraduate students on each campus, but in the state appropriation process no distinction is made.

Each campus has a chancellor, considerable autonomy in matters ranging from recruitment practices to faculty appointment packages, and substantial budgetary discretion. The campuses operate under a shared governance model where faculty and administration have joint responsibility and authority for decisions.

For most of the campuses in the system, enrollment growth will be a reality. Like faculty retirements, growth will play a significant role in faculty replacement needs on University of California campuses. On some campuses, it will be more important than the impact of retirement patterns, but not on the Berkeley and Los Angeles campuses, which have been designated, in the systemwide long-range development plan, as no-growth campuses.

To meet the enormous population growth in California (700,000 persons a year), the campuses at Davis, San Diego, and Irvine are each expected to reach 27,000 students by the year 2005. Santa Barbara, Santa Cruz, and Riverside also are slated to increase dramatically. The University of California system expects to enroll 221,350 students by the beginning of the next century and anticipates that in addition to growth plans at existing campuses, three new campuses will be needed to accommodate the demand expectation (see Table 6.1).

The anticipated increases in new faculty positions on the University of California campuses between academic year 1987–1988 and 2005–2006 are presented in Table 6.2, as are the numbers of expected retirements during the same time period. Changes in the mix of undergraduate and graduate students on the Berkeley campus will generate 25 new positions, and the campus can expect 902 retirements and 616 faculty separations for other reasons. The total number of appointments is estimated to be 1,543 faculty positions. In contrast, the San Diego campus, which was established in 1965, expects to need 1,340 faculty appointments, of which 564 will be new positions generated by growth in enrollments, 353 from retirements and 42

Table 6.1. Past and Projected Enrollments by Campus in the University of California System

Campus	1989	2005
Berkeley	30,510	29,450
Davis	21,147	26,850
Irvine	15,580	26,050
Los Angeles	34,005	34,500
Riverside	7,513	18,050
San Diego	16,797	26,750
Santa Barbara	17,952	20,000
Santa Cruz	9,305	15,000
San Francisco	3,599	4,000
Total	156,408	199,950[a]

[a] This total does not include all potential enrollees. Three new campuses are planned to accommodate an additional 21,400 students who are expected to enroll by the year 2005.

from other separations. The scenarios for Berkeley and San Diego may be different, but the tension of the new faculty drama is the same and the need is great.

Impetus to Examine the Policy Issue of Faculty Replacement

Faculty retirement issues including the aging of faculty members hired during the baby boom growth era and the Federal legislation eliminating the mandatory retirement age for faculty require a closer watch on retirement patterns. These issues coupled with the financial considerations of budget reductions and no enrollment growth provided the impetus for the examination of issues affecting faculty replacement.

Faculty Retirement. The Office of the President (systemwide administration) collects statistical information about existing and projected faculty needs on the campuses as part of its planning function. Because of anticipated changes over the next twenty years due to growth and retirements, the office has been actively monitoring these data.

In 1989–1990, there were 8,373 ladder-rank faculty in the University of California system, 173 retirements, and 167 other separations. Projections show that in 2005–2006 there will be 10,586 faculty; 4,042 retirements are expected, which is greater than historical retirement patterns. The cumulative statistic is dramatic, while the rate of turnover is constant.

The retirement picture will be augmented by the results of a recent retirement incentive program that increased faculty retirements unexpect-

Table 6.2. Anticipated Increases
in Faculty Positions and Numbers of Faculty Retirements
(1987-1988 to 2005-2006) in the University of California System

Campus	Net Increase in Positions	Retirements	Other Separations	Replacement Need	Total Number of Appointments
Berkeley	25	902	616	1,518	1,543
Davis	406	659	571	1,230	1,636
Irvine	608	213	368	581	1,189
Los Angeles	178	940	710	1,650	1,828
Riverside	543	206	241	447	990
San Diego	564	353	423	776	1,340
Santa Barbara	216	364	300	664	880
Santa Cruz	349	152	201	353	702
San Francisco	50	253	175	428	478
Total	2,939	4,042	3,605	7,647	10,586

Source: Office of Budget and Planning, University of California, Berkeley.

edly with the effect of moving forward the number of anticipated retirements. This retirement "bulge" has not yet been taken into account in systemwide projections.

A factor that may modify the "faculty demand" figure is the end of mandatory retirement; faculty who reach age 70 on or after July 2, 1993, will no longer be subject to a prescribed retirement date. This change in federal law has the potential for significantly affecting current retirement patterns on which future projections for faculty are based. In an effort to understand this impact, a systemwide survey was conducted of faculty not subject to mandatory retirement. It revealed that most faculty plan to retire between age 70 and 70.6 years, thus boosting the average retirement age from its current 66 years to about 68 years. However, 42 percent of faculty reported that the elimination of mandatory retirement did not affect their plans.

The survey results, while not definitive, suggest that the University of California can expect only a modest increase in the number of years that most faculty will continue to teach before retirement. However, a retirement "bulge" in 1991, which resulted from an early retirement incentive program means that for 1992–1995 there may be fewer retirements than projected.

Budget Reductions. A second and very significant factor affecting faculty position management is the availability of funds. Two successive years of state budget reductions have eroded the stability and the base of the university's operating budget. To alleviate the budget strain, an early retirement incentive program, called Plus 5, was offered to faculty and staff in 1990, and the university's program to "recall" retired faculty was improved so that the retirement incentive program did not jeopardize the teaching program.

The recall program allows a campus to offer retired faculty the opportunity to continue to teach courses in the respective departments. The department must initiate the recall, and the faculty member is limited to less than half-time employment on an annual contract. The intention was to reduce the number of expensive salary positions through retirement and replace the positions with less senior and/or less expensive people, thereby reducing faculty and staff personnel costs in the operating budget.

The Plus 5 program was funded by the university retirement system, not by the operating budget, and savings accrued from the retirements encouraged by Plus 5 were to be used for new faculty positions. However, because of state budget reductions, these savings were used instead to fill the gap between university expenses and state appropriations.

Steady State Enrollments. The decision that Berkeley maintain its current student enrollment level profoundly influences how the campus can plan for the future because increases in state appropriations are based on enrollment increases. This is a new and unfamiliar experience for Berkeley, the oldest campus in the University of California system, since it has experienced almost continuous growth during its history.

Reality of Existing Policy for Faculty Planning

Traditional faculty replacement practices could not continue in a period of budget reductions. Meeting faculty supply and demand needs and maintaining campus quality standards would require a more comprehensive understanding of faculty trends by discipline, including issues related to the faculty pipeline.

Practices and Procedures. The process for the allocation of faculty positions is followed routinely. Every two years departments prepare five-year academic plans that describe their expectations for future development and faculty replacements. Prior to 1991, it was accepted practice for departments to expect to replace any departing faculty member, and new departmental positions did not result from reallocations but from either growth or liens against impending retirements.

Beginning in the early 1980s a model for faculty replacements was used for allocation of new positions across campus. The model was driven by faculty separation rates and relied heavily on historical experience. It assumed a steady state enrollment picture and was not sensitive to changes in budget conditions, such as budget reductions. During the past decade, it was reasonably accurate because the campus budget was relatively stable. But budget stability is not the case today.

Influences and Considerations. In addition to factors affecting campuswide faculty retirements and funding constraints, faculty replacement planning on the Berkeley campus requires information on faculty needs by discipline and on faculty pipeline issues, including the recruitment of women and minority faculty. Data from a study of faculty replacement by discipline, conducted in 1990 by the University of California, Office of the President, Academic Affairs (see Table 6.3), show that 59 percent of the new faculty will be needed in the College of Letters and Sciences, and that the need is heavily concentrated in the humanities and social sciences. Among the professional schools, the demand for faculty in engineering and computer sciences will greatly exceed other disciplines. However, the dichotomy between the academy and professional schools may be misleading when considering faculty replacements. Academic faculty such as economists, political scientists, sociologists, and psychologists are increasingly being hired by business and law schools, forestry and agriculture schools, and schools of architecture and regional planning. The increasingly interdisciplinary nature of professional education blurs distinctions with respect to the schools, disciplines, and academic departments that will be competing for the same faculty.

Faculty replacement is very dependent on the availability of faculty. We have just emerged from nearly two decades of a tight job market for Ph.D. graduates, but it is obvious that nationally in the next decade faculty openings will exceed the production of new doctorates. In an effort to understand faculty pipeline issues, the Berkeley campus examined its production of doctoral graduates and discovered that during the job drought, the length of time to degree increased significantly. Further, comparisons with ten other research institutions showed similar experiences. Other findings included the following: time to degree is shorter at independent universities, women fail to complete graduate degrees at higher rates than men, and students in the humanities and social sciences consistently take a longer time to earn their degrees than do students in the physical and biological sciences.

These data, in combination with the fact that Berkeley produces the highest number of doctoral graduates in the United States (about eight hundred per year), have forced the Berkeley academic leadership to ask the following questions: Are independent universities providing better financial support for graduate students, thus limiting the number of years required for degree completion? What can be done to support women and increase their degree completion rates? Because the greatest need for faculty is in disciplines where production of faculty is slowest, what conscious efforts can be taken to reduce the time-to-degree rates? As both a consumer and a producer of faculty, Berkeley has a need and a responsibility to find the answers to these questions.

An additional issue influencing faculty replacement planning is faculty diversity. It may be more critical at Berkeley, which has a student body with no ethnic majority, but it also is a universal concern in American higher education. Efforts to recruit women and ethnic minorities have been only marginally successful, and students, legislators, advocacy groups, and faculty are intensifying demands to expand the gender and ethnic composition of the faculty. The supply to meet these demands is woefully inadequate in

Table 6.3. Projected Retirements by Field (1989–2008) at the University of California, Berkeley

Professional Schools and Colleges		Letters and Sciences	
Business Administration	26	Biological Sciences	69
Chemistry	33	Humanities	43
Education	21	Physical Sciences	94
Engineering and Computer Science	104	Social Sciences	132
Environmental Design	31	Ethnic Studies	4
Energy Resources Group	1		
Journalism	4		
Law	7		
Natural Resources	18		
Public Policy	2		
Social Welfare	7		
Health Sciences	26		
Total	307 (41%)		442 (59%) = 749

Source: Office of Budget and Planning, University of California, Berkeley.

many disciplines, and underutilized in other fields. The shortage of women and minorities prepared to take faculty positions creates a crisis for higher education, and it is the single most volatile issue in faculty replacement. The demands for women and minority faculty can be expected to persist. The situation will not be corrected except by a serious commitment to changing the available pool of potential faculty.

Realities and Visions

Budget reductions make it impossible to continue traditional faculty replacement practices. A more centralized approach to the management of faculty positions is needed, but the new model must take into consideration the Berkeley culture of a decentralized campus operation.

Changing Expectations. The budget reductions for fiscal years 1991 and 1992 made it impossible to continue business as usual at the Berkeley campus. But change was already in the making because of the steady enrollment state, a new administration, expected retirements, and increasing competition for faculty with sister campuses.

There are 1,786 budgeted faculty positions on the Berkeley campus. For budgetary flexibility, university policy requires campuses to assign at least 10 percent of budgeted faculty positions to temporary positions. In 1990–1991, there were 1,579 permanent faculty positions and 207 temporary positions assigned at Berkeley. Primarily as a result of the retirement incentive program, there has been an 11 percent reduction in senior faculty. In 1991–1992, the number of full professors decreased from 1,105 to 986, and the number of temporary faculty increased to 321. Much of the increase in temporary faculty can be attributed to the recall of retired faculty, but reliable data are not yet available to validate this observation.

Nearly all of the faculty who retired on the Plus 5 plan were over sixty-three years old. By taking advantage of the incentive program, faculty simply did in one year what had been expected to occur over five years. This concentrated number of retirements has created an unusually large number of unfilled permanently budgeted positions. It is a situation unlikely to be repeated, and it presents an opportunity to improve the planning and allocation processes for faculty positions.

Management Efforts. Berkeley's decentralized and collegial campus culture encourages consensus and discourages uniformity. Thus, it is not surprising that the management of faculty positions prior to 1991 was successful from the operational perspective but lacked cohesiveness from the institutional perspective. In 1991, the need to simultaneously address issues of faculty replacement, budget reductions, steady state enrollment, and affirmative action goals resulted in very specific actions.

Except for nontenured faculty positions, all vacated faculty positions will return to the central campus administration (the vice chancellor and the provosts) for reallocation. Department academic plans will be updated annually, and more emphasis will be put on the program reviews that are conducted periodically to evaluate the strengths, weaknesses, and needs of a department. The provosts have examined the relationship between undergraduate programs on campus and the course offerings in the professional schools, and shifts are taking place in course offerings to meet breadth requirements. A special assistant to the vice chancellor has been appointed to promote improvement in undergraduate education, and successful efforts have been made to encourage faculty to teach undergraduate seminars.

Initial efforts were directed toward generating better information about faculty positions. (The data presented in this chapter are an example.) The development of comprehensive faculty data is the outcome of serious concern by the systemwide administration for examining and understanding campus needs and the impact on the university system of campus management of faculty positions. On the Berkeley campus, a new budget process is being developed, including the management of faculty positions. Until the new process is completed, temporary faculty positions will not be shifted to permanent positions.

The vice chancellor has established a campuswide Academic Planning Board (APB) to complement existing efforts for planning, budgeting, and managing faculty positions. The APB was created to join the faculty and the administration in purposeful planning based on analysis and thoughtful consideration of current and projected conditions. Faculty and administration are equally represented on the APB.

The APB is responsible for reviewing quantitative and qualitative information on schools, departments, and programs. A data dictionary is being developed to provide information on each campus academic unit. The dictionary will include faculty position descriptions, student enrollment data by majors, funding sources and grant dollars, ethnographic details, graduate student outcomes data, contributions to campus excellence, and information on competitive faculty markets.

The APB will conduct program reviews focusing on long-term campus needs. Decisions affecting short-term needs will remain the prerogative of departments, deans, provosts, and the campus budget committee. The APB's objective is to act as a lens for the future, determining direction and establishing policy for the long-term character of the Berkeley campus. The APB charge is to recommend policies and priorities to the chancellor on campus programmatic needs. Policy analysis is the basic tenet on which the APB is designed to operate.

The new view that prevails is of a centralized campus, while respecting the decentralized nature of campus operations. It is hard to argue with the success of the Berkeley campus. Any changes necessary to face the new realities must respect the structures and dynamics that have made Berkeley's success possible, or the proposals will not be accepted.

Conclusion

Policy analysis for the management of faculty positions has been revitalized at Berkeley. The first step—better information and communication—has been taken and its processes will continue. Campus publications are now routinely used to inform and educate faculty and staff to the facts and the plans. The second step, development of strategies for improving the decision-making process surrounding the distribution of faculty positions, has begun. It will take time to see results, because faculty positions are approved a year in advance of their recruitment. But the process for managing faculty positions has begun. The third step, implementation of new practices, is underway. The systematic organization of information and a new forum for discussion are expected to refine current practices. There is no final step. The management of faculty positions is an activity dependent on dynamics that constantly change.

Although immediate realities have been the catalyst for reassessing faculty replacement planning, the goal of the Berkeley campus is to maintain the excellence of its faculty in meeting the mission of the University of California: teaching, research, and public service. The planning will be conscious, diligent, and as complex as the campus needs warrant.

References

Bowen, H. R., and Schuster, J. H. *American Professors: A National Resource Imperiled.* New York: Oxford University Press, 1986.

Bowen, W. G., and Sosa, J. *Prospects for Faculty in the Arts and Sciences: A Study of Factors Affecting Demand and Supply, 1987–2012.* Princeton, N.J.: Princeton University Press, 1989.

Chatman, S., and Jung, L. "Concern About Forecasts of National Faculty Shortages and the Importance of Local Studies." Paper presented at the 31st annual meeting of the Association of Institutional Research Forum, San Francisco, May 1991.

Gamson, Z. F., Finnegan, D. E., and Youn, T.I.K. *Assessing Faculty Shortages in Comprehensive Colleges and Universities.* New England Resource Center for Higher Education, Working Paper No. 2. Boston: University of Massachusetts, 1990.

ROSLYN R. ELMS was assistant vice chancellor at the University of California, Berkeley, and is now vice president for academic affairs at Northern Colorado University, Greeley.

The case studies in the preceding three chapters show how complex policy analysis can be.

An Analysis of Three Case Studies

Laura Saunders, Judith I. Gill

The case studies presented in Chapters Four through Six describe policy analysis activities in three higher education policy arenas: student enrollments, sexual harassment procedures, and faculty staffing. They illustrate different approaches to policy analysis as well as the breadth of policy analysis activities. This chapter uses the case studies to highlight the different components of policy analysis described in Chapter Two of this volume. Because the objectives, environments, and boundaries of the case studies are different, the attention given to each component will also be different across our reexaminations of the cases.

In each case study, the author was actively involved in the policy analysis activities. The authors share a comprehensive knowledge of higher education and of the environments of their case studies. Each author knew how to begin the required analysis activities, keep the project on track, and bring the analysis work to conclusion. In no case was the author an institutional researcher, but each depended on institutional research data and analysis.

One of the problems in using case studies to illustrate the process of policy analysis is that the case studies are written to present a complete view of the analytical problem, the issues, and the resolutions. The result is that the process of conducting policy analysis is often inferred but not highlighted. In this chapter, we draw attention to the policy analysis components that may be missed when reading for information on the policy problem.

Policy Analysis Tools

The policy analysis tools of iterative activity, intuition and judgment, and field testing are described in each case study. Jordan, in Chapter Four, is most explicit in describing the iterative nature of the policy analysis process; Olswang (Chapter Five) and Elms (Chapter Six) highlight the importance of judgment in understanding interdependent environmental components.

The Arizona University System's enrollment planning paradigm is based on the assumption that interdependent policies and practices affect student enrollment demand, and that enrollment projections cannot be based on simple calculations such as high school graduate projection rates. The paradigm's development included an investigation of factors affecting enrollment demand, discussions with university presidents on campus enrollment capacity, development of system strategies for meeting enrollment demands that included discussions with board members, and a review of the impact of different policy choices and the social consequences. Because each paradigm component is interdependent with other components, an iterative process of examining factors and their interrelationships was used in the development of the paradigm and will be used in its implementation.

Jordan's case study also highlights the use of field testing. In his chapter, a strong case is made for the benefits associated with gaining board member agreement on the statement of objectives, and the importance of gaining a better understanding of enrollment dynamics from discussions with university presidents.

Field-testing activities frequently provide opportunities for individuals who represent different groups with conflicting objectives to work through their differences. A key component for successful outcomes is a thorough understanding of the interdependent nature of the conflicting groups and good judgment in selecting the "right" people to participate in these activities. In the University of California case study, the vice chancellor established the campuswide Academic Planning Board to advise him on faculty replacement strategies, and faculty and administrators are equally represented on this board. At the University of Washington, the faculty senate chair and the university president appointed an administrator-faculty committee to review the broad system of due process on campus; the committee membership also included a representative from the state attorney general's office.

Diagnosing the Problem

A discussion of Stage 1 issues (objectives of analysis, understanding of the environment, understanding the boundaries and constraints, and initial statement) supports the importance of beginning the policy analysis assignment by developing an overview of the policy analysis task.

Objectives of Analysis. The first step in diagnosing a problem is to determine the objectives of the analysis. How have our authors addressed this task? Jordan identifies the need to develop a planning paradigm that can be used to understand issues affecting enrollment growth. The objective of analysis in the University of Washington case was to develop a due process procedure to protect the rights of faculty, students, and staff in investigations of sexual harassment complaints. And, at the University of California, Berkeley, the object of analysis was an examination of policies and practices affecting faculty replacement.

The Arizona University System faces the prospect of significantly increased enrollments. However, it lacks information on many factors affecting enrollment demand as well as on unintended and indirect consequences of an enrollment explosion. The objective of the policy analysis study was to develop a planning model that would provide the needed information.

The Arizona University System's new enrollment planning paradigm was built to meet four objectives: estimate enrollment to the year 2010, estimate optimum enrollment capacity, develop system strategies for meeting potential enrollment demands, and evaluate resource needs and potential funding sources. The intended outcome was to develop a model to project the student enrollment outcomes of given policy options.

The chapter on procedures for investigating sexual harassment complaints describes a case and process that gave rise to a reexamination of existing policy for handling accusations of sexual harassment at the University of Washington. The case study depicts the inadequacies of existing procedures that are based on traditional (faculty-only) collegial reviews. Policy analysis activities were involved in the development of recommendations for new procedures. The objectives were to provide for a more timely resolution of complex and controversial issues, and to ensure the due process rights of all persons in the dispute. The revised procedure was developed to meet these goals; it has not yet been tested.

The focus of policy analysis at the University of California at Berkeley was a study of factors influencing the management of faculty positions. This study was motivated by the changing faculty labor market, the large number of new openings and hiring opportunities due to retirements, and the need to recruit minority and women faculty in increasing numbers. Because of stable student enrollments at Berkeley and no anticipated growth in campus funding, each faculty vacancy was important campuswide, and departments and colleges could no longer be assured of maintaining their current number of faculty positions. Thus, the objectives for analysis were to develop a coherent strategy for maximum flexibility in managing faculty positions, as well as for some centralized direction in hiring decisions.

Not all of the parties in the case studies would necessarily agree with the authors' definitions of the objectives of analysis. However, in each case study, the author is a senior staff member for the principal policymaker(s), and thus the objectives described represent the policymakers' objectives.

Understanding the Environment. In each case study, environmental factors greatly influenced the direction of the policy analysis. In the enrollment planning study, the environmental factors are the dominant feature of the planning paradigm. They include not only demographic variables and institutional and state policies but also social and political trends and changes in institutional management strategies. In fact, much of the Jordan study is based on a new and broader definition of environmental factors affecting enrollment planning and forecasting.

The University of Washington case demonstrates the impact of public opinion and changing times on traditional faculty practices. As Olswang observes, "This case example demonstrates the obsolescence of the idea that loosely structured, faculty-only collegial reviews work in situations where a faculty member's job is at stake." Students and staff demanded fairness and due process in the review of their concerns involving faculty members.

Elms's description of the relationship between the campus and university system with respect to new faculty hires illustrates the complexities inherent to deriving policy for a campus within a system. An understanding of the environment and the interdependent themes is critical to the development of a new process for managing faculty positions. The interdependent environmental themes include the following: (1) Faculty retirements are an important part of a complex social matrix and cannot be reviewed as an isolated activity. (2) Student enrollments affect faculty replacement needs. (3) Race and gender are important considerations in faculty replacements. (4) Campus differences demand creative responses to the challenge of faculty replacement in a period of faculty shortages and restricted budgets.

Understanding Boundaries and Constraints. Boundaries and constraints for the three case studies include an understanding that the action plans were to be completed within a "reasonable" time period. Jordan needed to report back to the Arizona University System's Board of Regents; the new chancellor of the Berkeley campus wanted to move forward on his agenda for faculty before the state dollars became more limited and a limited supply of quality faculty was exhausted; and, at the University of Washington, new procedures needed to be in place before the next sexual harassment case was filed.

The reality of state funding limitations placed significant boundaries on the kind of recommendations that could be proposed for the Arizona University System and the University of California, Berkeley. Moreover, available and reliable data on high school graduation rates and immigration placed limitations on the statistical procedures that could be used in the Arizona planning model. Faculty retirement data, numbers of potential faculty by discipline, and California State revenue projections created problems for the design of information systems important to the management of faculty positions.

Many of the constraints in the University of Washington analysis focus on procedural boundaries and working relationships: the American Association of University Professors statement on due process and collegial procedures, American Council on Education guidelines, and existing procedures; social and contractual faculty expectations of how they will be treated; and administrative relationships between the dean and the university president. The University of California system policies for faculty represent boundary constraints for the Berkeley campus, and these constraints needed to be considered in the process of developing new campus policy. Additional constraints included the elimination of mandatory retirement requirements and the limited number of potential, high-quality ethnic and women faculty members.

Initial Statement. The importance of developing an initial statement is most clearly illustrated in the Arizona University System case study. Jordan and the chairman of the Strategic Planning Committee of the Board of Regents wrote a memorandum to the board enumerating the four principles of planning for enrollment growth. The memorandum included assumptions about growth and an extensive list of short- and long-term strategies that might be implemented to manage enrollment growth. The memorandum became the foundation on which the paradigm was built.

Unraveling the Policy Analysis Knot

The "real-world" application of the four principal components of policy analysis (policy issue, environment, implementation, and recommendations) are briefly reviewed in this discussion of the three case studies.

Policy Issue. Each author presents the policy issue as a key component of the case study: enrollment planning, procedures for investigating sexual harassment claims, and faculty supply and demand. Relevant studies providing key insights on the policy issue are identified at the end of each chapter. Jordan cites literature on enrollment trends and practices; Olswang provides a number of legal and procedural resources for the analyst; and Elms reviews studies on faculty supply and demand.

However, as these case studies demonstrate, in policy analysis the policy issue is secondary to an understanding of the environment and interdependent relationships among environmental variables.

Environment. The discussions of the environment are the foundation for the case studies. In Arizona, the demographics of a significant population increase, campus determination to downsize, and limited state resources depict an environment that will not easily accommodate the state's tradition of providing access to higher education at the student's campus of choice. The intricacies of faculty and administrative interaction over the procedural and due process issues at the University of Washington reflect the complexities of academic politics and policy. The reader can understand why the issues are so slow to be resolved given the number of committees and bodies that need to be consulted. Faculty hiring patterns and opportunities to hire new faculty are of central importance to the faculty, and the interplay between department and central administration goals in the California study contributes to the environment in which the policy analyst functions.

Implementation, Recommendations and Models, and Outcomes. Because policy analysis is conducted in the real world to address real-world problems and provide direction for their solutions, policy analysis must also carefully consider the implementation issues. If the analysis outcomes cannot be implemented in the real world, then the analysis is only academic and of limited use to the policymaker.

Jordan's development of a system dynamics model not only is a good example of a policy analysis outcome that can be implemented but also illustrates what an institutional researcher brings to policy analysis. The institutional researcher plays an important role in developing models that are data dependent. Arizona's enrollment demand model requirements include state demographic and economic data, tuition and fee data, student demographic data, college-going rates, enrollment rates, and census data.

Policy analysis activities were used in the development of the Arizona enrollment planning paradigm, and the outcome of this project is that the paradigm enables policy analysis to be conducted on enrollment-related policies and practices. The paradigm allows policymakers to plug in the "what if" questions and examine the impact of social and policy choices on enrollment demand, including the harmful or unintended outcomes.

At the University of Washington, the policy analysis outcome was the recommendation of a new model for investigating sexual harassment charges. The model provides for faculty consultation prior to the filing of a formal charge that could involve a decision to discipline a faculty member. However, a neutral party, not a faculty committee, would be responsible for carrying out the review process, and a panel of jurors would be impaneled. This panel would include peers of the victims (for example, a student or staff member) as well as peers of the accused.

The outcome of an analysis of policies and practices affecting faculty staffing on the Berkeley campus was the creation of the campuswide Academic Planning Board, and the development of a comprehensive faculty data base that includes descriptions of faculty positions, student enrollment data by majors, data on funding sources and grant dollars, ethnographic details, graduate student outcomes data, contributions to campus excellence, and information on long-term campus needs.

Conclusion

The case studies represent interim outcomes of the policy issues. Because the environment is not static, issues will repeat themselves, and very seldom are there any truly final outcomes for the policy analyst.

These case studies dealt with assumptions and revisions, the complexity and evolving nature of policy analysis, and the presentation of an outcome for the policymaker. While they describe vastly different kinds of policy analysis, they have in common the iterative, repetitive approach to analysis that results in recommendations that can be implemented because they fit the environment from which they emerged.

LAURA SAUNDERS is dean of administration at Highline Community College, Des Moines, Washington.

JUDITH I. GILL is director of research and policy analysis for the Western Interstate Commission for Higher Education.

A university president provides advice to policy analysts. He emphasizes that the successful analyst understands administrative realities.

Confessions of a Researcher Turned Policymaker

Kenneth P. Mortimer

The title of this chapter seems to suggest that policymakers who have been researchers or analysts somehow have gone astray, that is, that there is something to "confess." The line between an analyst and a practitioner often is not clear. Analysts often act as consultants to policymakers and sometimes themselves move in and out of the role of policymaker. Policy analysts can get impatient with the failure of policymakers to follow their advice and become motivated to try to set policy themselves. And, of course, practitioners get equally concerned about the inability of analysts to tell it like it is, and so they take up the role of analyst.

I confess that my intellectual background has spanned the roles of analyst as well as policymaker. My undergraduate majors are English and political science. I earned an M.B.A. and did graduate work in political science and public administration before completing a Ph.D. in the administration of higher education. I was a faculty member in a higher education program from 1969 to 1984, and in public administration from 1981 to 1984. For five years I served as a part-time director of a research center, and I also served as a consultant to over two dozen institutions. Since 1984, I have been engaged in full-time administration, first as a vice president and vice provost, and, since 1988, as president of Western Washington University.

In short, the study and practice of administration has been my delight for about twenty-five years. In my current role as a practitioner, I have been asked to advise analysts who want to influence policy. This chapter is based on this advice and has essentially three parts. First, I discuss some of the basic criticism of researchers in higher education who seek to influence policy-making. Second, I write about the administrative realities that, in my opinion, tend not to be understood by those who conduct research and policy analysis on higher education. Finally, I offer advice to researchers who want to be influential in the policy-making process. The basis for the advice and counsel offered is personal experience.

The Critics

Daniel T. Layzell (1990) offers an articulate analysis of why higher education research fails to influence administrators. He suggests that a basic criterion for judging the effectiveness of policy analysis should be whether or not researchers speak to the pressing problems confronting administrators today. These he identifies as cost containment, service to diverse populations, accountability and assessment, economic development, finances, student financial aid, governance, tuition, and student costs.

His basic analysis is that research tends to come up short when judged against the standard of whether it speaks effectively to the pressing problems of the day. He characterizes most of the policy analysis efforts that go on in higher education programs as dry and pedestrian.

He offers good advice to policy analysts who want to be influential. He urges an emphasis on issues that are of interest to policymakers and on the big picture rather than microproblems. The reader is further advised to conduct more comparative studies, to deemphasize research methodology in the treatment of problems, and to use less higher education jargon in analysis and presentation. In short, analysts are advised to put their heads where the higher education practitioner's head is, to be more straightforward, and to communicate results more clearly without specific reference to confusing methodologies. For the most part, these criticisms are valid.

Administrative Realities

The criticism of analysts such as Layzell needs to be put in the context of the policy-making environment of administrators. Here, I refer essentially to presidents and vice presidents rather than to department or college administrators. I can offer seven sets of observations about administrative realities based on my experience as vice president at Pennsylvania State University and president at Western Washington University.

Power and Influence of the Board of Trustees. Almost everyone internal to the university underestimates the power and influence of a board of trustees on a president and the cabinet. Most presidents understand very well that the board of trustees is the boss, and that whatever the policy limits that he or she is considering, they have to be judged in the context of whether or not the board will find them acceptable.

Even in sacred discussions of individual promotion and tenure cases, boards of trustees' expectations vary immensely depending on the tradition and culture of the institution and the appropriate role of trustees in such decisions. In some states, trustees discuss individual promotion and tenure decisions "in the sunshine," while other boards delegate such matters to the administration.

One or two examples of board influence might lend meaning to this observation. In one institution, during the debate in the 1980s about university investments in South Africa, the university community put immense public pressure on the administration to divest its investment portfolio of companies doing business in South Africa. The administration went to great lengths to explain and defend current policy in support of the so-called Sullivan Principles. The internal decision-making process of the administration was heavily governed by the members of the board of trustees who supported the Sullivan Principles with great conviction. The board took several votes on the issue, and there was no hope that the administration could change board views on this particularly important public debate.

Many university communities are unaware of the extent to which a president and other members of the institutional leadership have to anticipate likely trustee opinion so that recommendations sent to the trustees will be the ones that the board can accept. The process of bringing acceptable recommendations to the board sometimes is subtle, whereas at other times it is governed by specific board direction.

I have been involved in the handling of student sit-ins in two different institutions, one where the board had a policy of not allowing sit-ins to remain in the building overnight, and another in which the board let the administration decide appropriate policy. The first situation led to mass arrests of students, and the other resulted in the students occupying the building for two nights and then leaving the building of their own accord on the third day. Board policy was the determining feature in each of these cases.

Insufficient Time to Attend to All Issues. There is never enough time to devote to all of the wide range of issues confronting a president and vice presidents. Wise administrators know that one of the most important factors in their effectiveness is the issues to which they decide to attend. And the span of attention is a forced choice, since there are more stimuli than one can possibly absorb.

A large institution, such as a public research university, may have over one hundred pieces of mail a day come into the president's office. The way in which that flow of information is directed, molded, and shaped is very important in deciding what gets handled personally by the president and what gets directed to others in the institution.

Overall, these leaders have to operate on past experience and intuition to tell them what is important, what requires their personal attention, and what can safely be directed to others. In many cases, that initial decision as to what the president sees is determined by an executive assistant. It is only a slight exaggeration to say that university presidents read only what they have to in order to do their jobs and that they need to be careful about which issues they ignore.

Need to Understand the Importance of Ceremonies and Symbols. It is important to spend time shaking hands, smiling at people, and saying kind words at appropriate moments. Because these matters are so important, they consume an inordinate amount of time. This compounds further the problem of a policy analyst who is concerned about issues rather than processes and/or symbols. Yet, symbols and processes can be as important as the substance of an issue.

Sometimes an issue so rapidly achieves importance that there is no time to study alternatives, but action is required almost immediately. I became president of Western Washington University on September 15, 1988, as the fall quarter was starting. The Admissions Office informed me that we were overenrolled and that there were several legislative penalties that the institution would suffer as a consequence. There was no time to study or conduct analyses of the enrollment situation; this was a situation that required immediate attention.

Administrative Accountability. When a policy analyst recommends a course of action and it is followed but does not work, the researcher is off on another project and the policymaker is left to clean up the mess. There is no escape from the final responsibility for things that go well or ill. Further, things that may appear correct from an analytical point of view may not work when politics and personalities are considered.

One of the more interesting adventures in my career as a faculty member was when I participated in the demise of a faculty club. Previous market studies had "proved" that a faculty club could be sustained at the institution. The study showed that approximately one thousand faculty members would join the club and that they would be willing to pay dues of around $100 a year. In practice, when the club opened it was only able to recruit five hundred members, and there was a lot of price cutting in order to arrive at that level. In other words, there was a general unwillingness to pay $100 a year in dues. These two facts were major causes for closure of the club within two years.

Another instance of the gulf between principle and practice occurred when I served as a consultant to the University of California in 1971. The basic issue that I was asked to analyze was how to organize the extended university work within the nine-campus University of California system. The university was interested in developing off-campus and extended degree programs, which were sweeping the country in the early 1970s, probably stimulated by the success of the Open University in the United Kingdom. My analytical work involved a month-long series of visits to each of the nine campuses in the university system. I discussed organizational models and the political realities of the University of California with various campus administrators and faculty members involved in the various extended operations of the university.

I became persuaded that the extended university concept would not work within the structure of the existing nine-campus system. I recommended that the university create a tenth unit without a campus. In my opinion, the resistance to an extended university within each of the nine campuses would make it very difficult, if not impossible, for the extended university to succeed within the University of California system.

In retrospect, I believe that I was right in my analysis but wrong in my understanding of the politics of the University of California in the early 1970s. It simply was not possible to create a tenth campus for the extended university. In short, I was analytically correct but politically wrong.

A third example is the development of branch campuses in the state of Washington during the 1980s. Policy analysts rightly pointed out that the state of Washington was underserved at the upper-division and graduate levels. Several analysts argued that the most effective way to provide greater access to underserved areas such as the cities of Tacoma, Vancouver, Seattle, and Spokane and the Tri-Cities region was to replicate the regional university concept. Regional universities can concentrate on upper-division and master's degree programming in a more cost-effective manner than can the alternative—research universities—since their costs per student are lower.

There were several political realities that eventually controlled the solution adopted by the Higher Education Coordinating Board and eventually the legislature in the state of Washington. One of the political realities was simply that the twenty-seven community colleges and their board would not allow the founding of any more four-year colleges or universities in the state. The community colleges support an approach to upper-division education that concentrates on admission of the graduates of the community college transfer programs, rather than admission of students as freshmen to study at a university or college for four-year baccalaureate degrees. Any new institutions were likely to be limited to upper-division and graduate education. A second political reality was that communities asked about their preferences came down very strongly in favor of research as opposed to regional universities. The prestige factor of having a branch of a research university, as opposed to a regional university, is very important in the policy-making process. The communities wanted a campus of the university, not a regional teacher's college.

The eventual solution was the creation of five branch campuses that offer programs at the upper-division and graduate levels only. These branch campuses are affiliated with Washington State University and the University of Washington. In effect, the regional universities have been prevented from providing greater access, largely for prestige reasons. Some analysts cite this development as the triumph of wants (prestige) over needs (less costly delivery systems).

Dangers of the Rumor Mill. The president is not free to speculate or wonder in public about specific alternatives or courses of action. Administrative speculations about alternatives quickly fuel the rumor mill and lead to defensive behavior and/or aggressive reaction by the affected parties.

In one of my early discussions with faculty about strategic planning, I was asked to give examples of academic programs that could be considered outside the core disciplines that are required to be in place at any major university. I used the example of theater to point out how different universities conceive of disciplines in quite different ways. Some universities view theater as literature and offer coursework under the auspices of their English departments. Such was the case when I majored in English at the University of Pennsylvania in the 1960s. Other universities view theater as performance and have full-fledged departments of theater, normally located in the College of Fine Arts or its equivalent.

So, I ventured the opinion that one could not conceive of a university without an English department, or of a university that did not have some theater somewhere in its curriculum. I could, however, conceive of a university without a department of theater. The rumor mill reported that I was prepared to close the theater department at Western Washington University!

In light of this lack of freedom to engage in speculative conversation, academic policymakers should require policy analysts to develop alternative courses of action. When creating a unit devoted to the study of communications at one university, we required the committee to give us alternative organizational configurations. So, when we were considering the committee report on this issue, we had five different configurations and, in our ingenuity, we actually adopted a combination of elements of all of them. In other words, we created a sixth alternative.

In another situation, we had already decided to merge two colleges, and we asked the committee not to develop alternatives but rather to recommend how to merge the colleges and to assess what the impact of the merger might be on the institution and its programs. The committee report helped us to achieve a relatively smooth merger.

Problems in Implementing Policy Recommendations. While policy analysts spend a great deal of time deciding on *what* course of action to follow, administrators spend an equally great portion deciding on *how* to accomplish something after a course of action is determined. For example, most administrators in research universities would give their life savings if somebody could give them a sure-fire recipe about how to get faculty to pay more attention to students. When the committee I was on was preparing *Involvement in Learning: Realizing the Potential of American Higher Education* (National Institute of Education, 1984), we were convinced that a group of reasonably intelligent researchers and analysts could develop a set of principles that would improve the quality of the undergraduate experience. The major problem with such principles is how to get them implemented: how to get university administrators and faculties involved in encouraging more active forms of learning, more effective forms of assessment and feedback about that learning, in an atmosphere of raised expectations and standards. All of those nice words are confounded by the simple fact that it is very difficult to translate them into a plan of action and then to implement the plan.

Administrative Myopia. Involvement in administration for extended periods of time creates or encourages an incapacity to see relationships and possibilities. The mere fact that one has been an administrator for fifteen or twenty years colors the acceptance of policy research that is not consistent with past experiences.

This danger first became apparent to me in the early 1970s when higher education was debating the impact of public employee collective bargaining laws on academic governance. Some of the debate hinged on which aspects of the industrial experience in collective bargaining could be applied to higher education. A number of higher education administrators were arguing that since universities were communities of scholars and not adversarial organizations with highly developed canons of conflicts of interest, the traditional collective bargaining model was inappropriate. Those experienced in collective bargaining in the industrial sector and in teachers' unions in the public schools argued that the model was flexible enough to be adapted to any organization and that universities were no different in this respect.

The argument at that time was over different conceptual approaches to dispute resolution in the context of academe. Labor lawyers and other experienced collective bargaining practitioners were operating with a conceptual lens that was focused on the appropriate ways to resolve disputes in organizations. They did not seem to understand that the *method* of dispute resolution was the focus of the debate. Higher education administrators and traditionalists were simply arguing that arbitration and other forms of dispute resolution consistent with the industrial experience had very little, if any, place in the higher education environment of the early 1970s. There was a basic difference in conceptual lenses, with advocates of collective bargaining persuaded that higher education was no different from any other type of organization, and the opponents persuaded that the university was such a special organization that traditional practices in dispute resolution would not fit.

A second major example of the trained myopia that tends to color debates in higher education is arguments about costs. Economists and accountants argue about the various definitions of cost that turn up on balance sheets or in various allocation formulas produced by state legislatures and coordinating boards. These definitions of cost have very useful applications in higher education but do not explain the reality that Howard Bowen (1977) and David Breneman have articulated so well.

Bowen's discussions of higher education encompass four basic observations about costs in the policy-making environment. First, Bowen hypothesizes that the dominant goals of universities are power, prestige, and quality and/or excellence, and that there is no limit to the amount of money that can be spent in pursuit of these goals. (Does one ever have enough prestige, power, or quality?)

Second, administrators in higher education raise all the money that they can, and they spend all that they raise. The overwhelming impact of these behaviors is to increase costs. Since there is no limit to the amount of money that can be spent in pursuit of the dominant but ambiguous goals, the overwhelming trend is to raise more money and spend more money and therefore increase costs!

Third, the nebulous nature of costs in higher education is exacerbated by the great debate over the use of formulas in public resource allocations. Most of the discussion about formulas is based on how to allocate whatever money is eventually appropriated by the legislature. The legislature continues to debate the total dollars available. Most administrators would be happy indeed if necessary costs were somehow related to the dollars provided.

Fourth, very seldom is the discussion of costs in higher education geared toward actually determining how much money is required to educate a given number of students. David Breneman illustrates the nebulous nature of cost discussions when he describes the tuition-setting process in many independent liberal arts colleges. He argues that tuition levels in many colleges are not a function of increased costs but rather of increased pricing discussions and the institution's estimate of its niche in the marketplace in which it seeks to compete. Many independent colleges have come to realize that students do not make a decision to attend a given college because it is $200 or $300 or even $500 less expensive than a rival. Once this point is understood, decisions to engage in price warfare on the margins will become ineffective.

A final illustration of administrative myopia is in the area of budget and resource allocation and space allocation in universities and colleges. First as an analyst and then as a practitioner, I have sat through twenty to twenty-five budget and space hearings a year, at two institutions, over a period of eight years. This experience tends to make the eyes glaze over and results in an informal set of attitudes and opinions about how to cope with seemingly limitless requests for more money and/or space.

During one of those years, I was privileged to know several of the newly appointed faculty members to the budget committee. These were intelligent colleagues who were sophisticated about university governance but were having their first experiences with universitywide budget matters. One of them took me aside after the first round of hearings and asked, "How much of what I am hearing can I believe?" I replied that one can believe everybody who is in these budget sessions, and that they would spend every penny that was given to them. Beyond that, it was a matter of judgment and priorities to be sorted out by loosely drawn criteria. Given the nebulous nature of resource and space allocation judgments in universities, the administrators who participate annually in this pull-and-tug develop attitudes and have a hardness of opinion that makes it difficult to internalize the findings of many analytical studies.

Advice to Analysts

Having looked at both the criticism of policy analysts and my own analysis of the administrative realities that most analysts tend not to take into account, I can offer three general observations for analysts. First, in spite of the critics, it is important for several reasons to keep methodological and conceptual rigor in policy analysis: (1) Most policy analysts work within the context of universities and/or professional associations that are dominated by university faculty. Methodological and conceptual rigor is absolutely crucial to credibility in this context. (2) External validity and comparative efforts are advanced by methodological rigor, and these are important ingredients to the extent that they affect practitioners' willingness to accept the policy analyst's results.

While I continue to urge methodological and conceptual rigor, I also urge that the documents and reports prepared for administrators not be dominated by excessive treatments of methodology. Given the administrative reality that there is never enough time to complete everything that needs to be done, recognize that administrators will read summaries and read *at*, rather than *digest*, extensive amounts of analytical work.

Second, policy analysts have to decide individually whether influence on higher education policy is important both to them and to the unit in which they are working. Much of the literature in higher education concentrates on illumination of major philosophical and conceptual issues confronting policymakers. Sometimes the history of higher education or the history of an issue, such as who should pay for higher education, is not of basic interest to administrators. Yet, one cannot demean the importance of such studies to the evolution of general higher education policy. Those who choose to illuminate such issues must be comforted in other ways than by being influential with policymakers.

Finally, perhaps one of the more difficult tasks for policy analysts is to assume the responsibility of an institutional researcher. Here, one has the responsibility to be methodologically rigorous and conceptually sound, and yet responsible for shedding light on issues that do not readily lend themselves to rigor and soundness. Our profession would be improved if we could help educate policymakers about how to frame intelligent questions and help them to understand the limitations of policy analysis in dealing with political dilemmas.

References

Bowen, H. *Investment in Learning: The Individual and Social Value of American Higher Education.* San Francisco: Jossey-Bass, 1977.

Layzell, D. T. "Most Research on Higher Education Is Stale, Irrelevant, and of Little Use to Policy Makers." *Chronicle of Higher Education,* Oct. 24, 1990, pp. B1, B3.

National Institute of Education. *Involvement in Learning: Realizing the Potential of American Higher Education.* Washington, D.C.: National Institute of Education and U.S. Department of Education, 1984.

KENNETH P. MORTIMER *is president of Western Washington University, Bellingham.*

What lies ahead? This chapter presents tips on building an effective policy analysis capability.

The Agenda Ahead

Laura Saunders, Judith I. Gill

Armed with a road map for conducting policy analysis, the analyst's work can begin. There are challenges ahead, however, and most difficult for institutional researchers venturing into the policy arena is the task of assessing whether policy recommendations can be implemented. Tests of the feasibility of implementing recommendations and a determination of what economists call "spillover" effects lead the institutional researcher deep into institutional culture and folkways. Tests of models and data gathering are straightforward compared to the task of determining whether the faculty, the legislature, or a vocal lobbying group will find a set of recommendations satisfactory.

Development of the capability to conduct good policy analysis begins in the same way as development of the capability to conduct institutional research studies or prepare institutional plans. Begin with scholarly research training, add an increasing familiarity with the professional literature, and supplement both with quality discussions among colleagues—this recipe provides the analyst with the necessary knowledge for collecting data and critiquing current literature. The development of skill in assessing the implementation feasibility of policy recommendations is partially the result of careful analysis and study, but it is equally important to develop an understanding of the institutional histories of policy issues.

In some respects, policy analysis is similar to writing a newspaper story or documenting an institutional history. Institutional researchers can call upon the skills of librarians, public relations directors, and legislative liaison staff in gathering this necessary but perhaps elusive background information. Similar to training in gathering data for a story, learning to ask the right questions is as important in policy analysis as it is in recording the history of an event.

Another component useful to building the capacity to do good analysis is familiarity with the setting. By serving on institutional committees and meeting with faculty, staff, alumni, and students on an informal basis, policy analysts can add to their knowledge base. Intuition may be an inborn capability, but knowledge about the setting shapes judgment and increases the probability that recommendations will fit the environment. Particularly in large, complicated institutions, where there are different organizational entities whose members meet each other only in the parking lot, familiarity with internal political struggles provides invaluable background information. Recent work in the anthropology of higher education, such as Tierney's (1991) detailed discussion of the ethnographic interview, offers suggestions on how to develop interviewing and observation skills.

The public debate on the role, nature, and function of higher education is another environmental influence on policy analysis. Good policy analysis refines and redirects that debate and, in so doing, leads to better policy-making. A striking feature of this approach is the iterative nature of policy analysis: Environmental factors give rise to policy issues requiring analysis and leading to recommendations, the implementation of which leads to environmental changes and a new version of the policy issue.

Another aspect of developing the capability for conducting effective policy analysis is the establishment of an appropriate field-testing team. The analyst should quickly identify those individuals on campus, or in governing board offices, whose knowledge and support are key to an understanding of the issues and to the eventual adoption of recommendations. Governmental affairs and public relations staff are particularly useful in field-testing initial formulations and recommendations, for their wide experience in the extra-institutional environment well equips them to assess the practical impact of policy. A variety of individuals and points of view need to be identified, and each person consulted as part of the field-testing team should be queried about others whose assessments may be crucial.

Tips on the Road to Good Analysis

The bottom line of policy analysis is that it is a decision-making tool. Policy analysis exists in the real world of decisions, decision makers, limited time, and limited resources. Policy analysis is every bit as messy as the real world. An understanding of the higher education environment is the key to good analysis. In addition, we offer the following tips:

1. Recognize personal biases when conducting analysis.
2. Be flexible and inclusive.
3. Be realistic but creative in framing recommendations.
4. Build an advisory team who will say what they really think.
5. Do not get frustrated by the number of repetitions.

6. Look at the forest and then look at the trees and then look back at the forest.
7. Implementation is the key to good policy.
8. Do not surprise the institution's president.

Sources for Help

The Pew Memorial Trust has published the series *Policy Perspectives,* which captures some of the important policy discussions now occurring in higher education. The *Chronicle of Higher Education, Public Administration Review,* and the bibliographical publications from the Association for Higher Education are also excellent sources for discussion of current policy issues, as well as descriptions of the educational environment.

Much of the literature of higher education is the so-called fugitive literature—occasional publications and papers that circulate from office to office. The task of locating copies of this literature requires persistence, as well as the use of the increasingly popular electronic communications networks. The institutional researcher is probably already familiar with the Association for Institutional Research electronic newsletter, but a similar newsletter for planners and rapidly forming and expanding discussion groups on topics such as community colleges, assessment, and Total Quality Management add to the available resources.

Reference

Tierney, W. G. "Utilizing Ethnographic Interviews to Enhance Academic Decision Making." In D. M. Fetterman (ed.), *Using Qualitative Methods in Institutional Research.* New Directions for Institutional Research, no. 72. San Francisco: Jossey-Bass, 1991.

LAURA SAUNDERS is dean of administration at Highline Community College, Des Moines, Washington.

JUDITH I. GILL is director of research and policy analysis for the Western Interstate Commission for Higher Education.

INDEX

Academe, 35
Academic Planning Board, University of California (Berkeley), 65, 68
Accountability: of policymakers, 80–91; for state funds, 26
Accreditation requirements, 23
Administration. *See* Governance; Policy making; Presidents; Public administration
Admissions, differentiated, 43
Advisers, in policy analysis, 16; panel of, 17; pros and cons of, 18. *See also* Field testing
Age, and enrollment projections, 41
Alexander v. Yale University, 50
Allocation. *See* Funding;Resources
Alternatives, importance of, 82
Alumni Research: Methods and Applications, 34
American Association of University Professors (AAUP), 49, 55, 56, 70
American Council on Education, 49, 56, 70
Applying Statistics in Institutional Research, 34
Arizona State University-West Campus, 44
Arizona University System, 18; enrollment planning in, 37–47, 68, 70, 71, 72; governance system in, 44. *See also* University of Arizona
Assessing Academic Climates and Cultures, 34–35
Assessment, and minority student participation, 35
Association for Higher Education, 87
Association for Institutional Research (AIR), 29
Assumptions, identification of, 21
Attrition rates, study of, 32. *See also* Enrollment planning
Austin, A., 35

Balderston, F. E., 5, 6, 8, 9, 10, 11, 12, 13
Beckman, N., 5, 6, 7, 8, 9, 10, 11, 12
Behavioral/nonbehavioral decision making, 10

Bensimon, E. M., 35
Board of Regents v. *Roth,* 53
Board of Trustees, influence of, 76–78
Boundaries/limits, in policy analysis. *See* Constraints
"Bounded rationality," policy analysis as, 8
Bowen, H., 57, 66, 81–82, 83
Bowen, W. G., 57, 66
Braybrooke, D., 6, 7, 8, 9, 12
Breneman, D., 81, 82
Brinkman, P. T., 34, 35
Budget decision making: and allocation, 82–83; and Planning-programming-budgeting-system, 5
Budget reductions, effect of on faculty staffing, 60, 61, 62, 64, 70. *See also* Funding; Resources

Campbell, D., 49, 56
Campuses: branch, 44, 79; expansion of, 44. *See also* Physical plant; Sexual harassment
Case studies, for illustrating policy analysis, 67. *See also* Enrollment planning; Faculty position management; Sexual harassment
Cates, C., 6, 7, 11, 12
Ceremony, importance of, 78
Change. *See* Modification
Chatman, S., 57, 66
Chronicle of Higher Education, 34, 87
Civil Rights Act of 1964, Title VII, 50
Coleman, J. S., 6, 9, 11, 12
Collective bargaining, in academic institution, 81
Community colleges: and cooperation with state university system, 38, 39, 43; and cross-registration, 45–46; increasing transfer rates from, 45–46; politics of, 79
Computer simulation modeling approach, 39
Conducting Interinstitutional Comparisons, 34
Conflict: and field testing, 68; about intended outcomes, 19; about policy recommendations, 26. *See also* Politics

89

gies in, 9; models for, 10–11; compared with planning, 32–33; and policy outcomes, 11; process of, 18–27, 71–72; tips for success in, 75–83, 86–87; tools for, 7–8, 16, 17–18, 67–68. *See also* Higher education; Policy implementation
Policy implementation, 11, 16, 22; in case studies, 72; factors affecting, 25–26; and feasibility assessment, 85; problems in, 80–81. *See also* Outcomes; Policy making; Recommendations
Policy issues. *See* Issues
Policy making, 3, 11; and defining analysis objectives, 19; and environmental factors, 76–83; and initial statement of analysis, 18; and successful policy analysis, 75–83. *See also* Decision making; Presidents
Policy research. *See* Issues
Political science, policy analysis in, 7, 9
Politics, as factor in policy analysis, 17, 24–25, 26, 31, 78. *See also* Conflict; Constraints; Environment; Political science
Pragmatism, in policy analysis, 8
Prediction, and policy analysis, 11
Presidents, institutional: administrative issues of, 76–83; myopia of, 81–82; and policy recommendations, 26
Primer on Institutional Research, A, 29
Problem diagnosis, in policy analysis, 18–22; case study illustrations of, 68–71
Public administration: curriculum of, 5–6; policy analysis and, 75–83; problems of, 76. *See also* Governance; Presidents
Public Administration Review, 87
Public service, by state university system, 38

Quade, E. S., 6, 7, 8, 9, 11, 13
Qualitative analysis, 9–10, 31
Quantitative analysis/modeling, 9, 10, 31
Questionnaires, resources on, 34

Rand Corporation, 6
Rational-comprehensive model, 10
Recessions, effect of on higher education, 24, 41

Recommendations, from policy analysis, 22–23, 25–27, 31. *See also* Outcomes; Policy implementation
Regional universities, 79
Repetition, in policy analysis, 16. *See also* Iterative process
Report. *See* Written report
Research: academic, 6; in state university system, 38
Research universities, 79
Resources: allocation of, 82–83; and policy analysis, 8, 16, 21. *See also* Budget; Constraints
Responding to New Realities in Funding, 34
Riger, S., 49, 56
Robertson, C., 49, 56
Rumors, dangers of, 79–80
Ryan, J., 49, 56

Salancik, G. R., 8, 9, 13
Saunders, L., 1–3, 5, 15, 29, 67, 85
Saupe, J. L., 29, 36
Schick, A., 11, 13
Schneider, B. E., 49, 56
Schuster, J. H., 57, 66
"Science of Muddling Through, The," 5
Sexual harassment cases: analysis of procedures in, 2–3, 18, 49–56; case example of, 50–53; constraints on policy analysis of, 70; as discrimination, 50; environmental factors in, 70; incidence of, 49; laws regarding, 50; new models for, 54–55; objectives of policy analysis for, 69; outcomes of policy analysis for, 72; publicity of, 51, 53; traditional procedures in, 49–50, 53–55
Simon, H. A., 8, 13
Smith, B.L.R., 7, 13
Social consequences, of enrollment policy choices, 45. *See also* Enrollment planning
Social sciences, and policy analysis, 24
Sosa, J., 57, 66
Stages, of policy analysis process, 18–27
State population growth, 41, 59
Statistical methodologies, in policy analysis, 9, 34. *See also* Methodologies
Steady state enrollment, 61

ORDERING INFORMATION

NEW DIRECTIONS FOR INSTITUTIONAL RESEARCH is a series of paperback books that provides planners and administrators in all types of academic institutions with guidelines in such areas as resource coordination, information analysis, program evaluation, and institutional management. Books in the series are published quarterly in Spring, Summer, Fall, and Winter and are available for purchase by subscription as well as by single copy.

SUBSCRIPTIONS for 1992 cost $45.00 for individuals (a savings of 20 percent over single-copy prices) and $60.00 for institutions, agencies, and libraries. Please do not send institutional checks for personal subscriptions. Standing orders are accepted.

SINGLE COPIES cost $14.95 when payment accompanies order. (California, New Jersey, New York, and Washington, D.C., residents please include appropriate sales tax.) Billed orders will be charged postage and handling.

DISCOUNTS FOR QUANTITY ORDERS are available. Please write to the address below for information.

ALL ORDERS must include either the name of an individual or an official purchase order number. Please submit your order as follows:
   Subscriptions: specify series and year subscription is to begin
   Single copies: include individual title code (such as IR1)

MAIL ALL ORDERS TO:
   Jossey-Bass Publishers
   350 Sansome Street
   San Francisco, California 94104

FOR SALES OUTSIDE OF THE UNITED STATES CONTACT:
   Maxwell Macmillan International Publishing Group
   866 Third Avenue
   New York, New York 10022